3/09

# FIRST IN SPACE

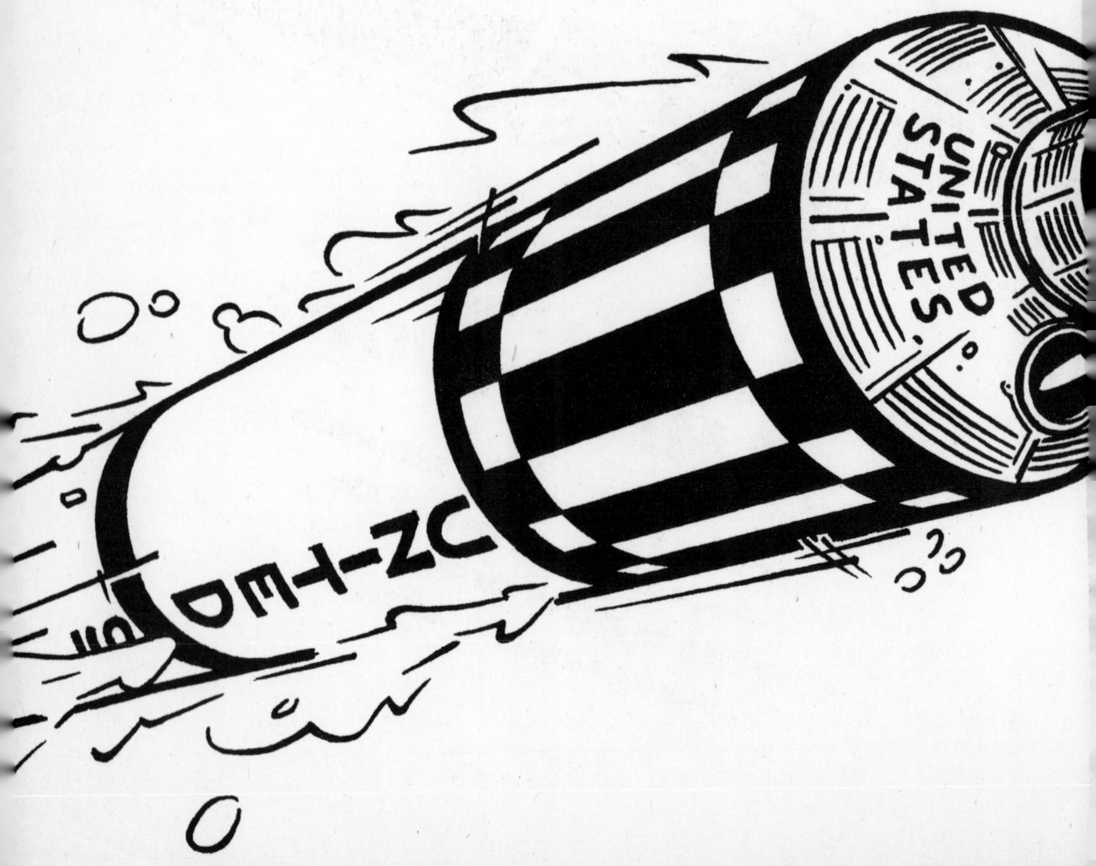
UNITED STATES

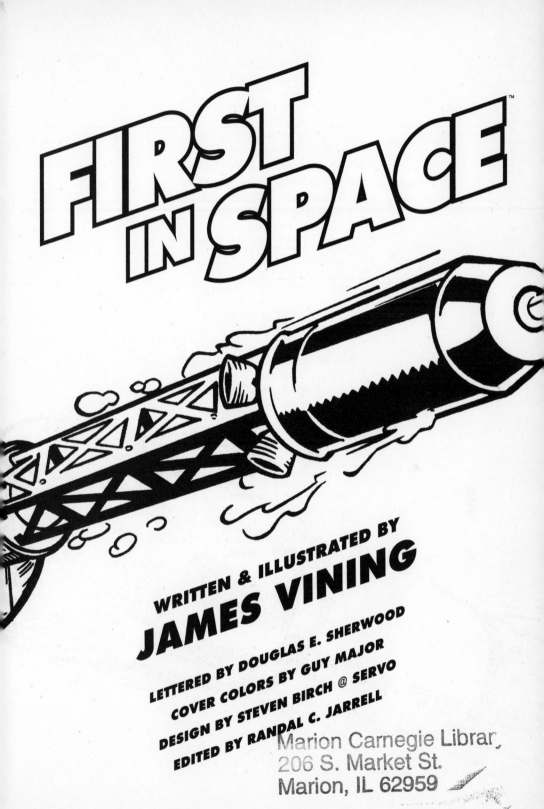

# FIRST IN SPACE™

WRITTEN & ILLUSTRATED BY
## JAMES VINING

LETTERED BY DOUGLAS E. SHERWOOD
COVER COLORS BY GUY MAJOR
DESIGN BY STEVEN BIRCH @ SERVO
EDITED BY RANDAL C. JARRELL

Published by Oni Press, Inc.
Joe Nozemack, publisher
James Lucas Jones, editor in chief
Randal C. Jarrell, managing editor
Doug Sherwood, editorial assistant
Jill Beaton, editorial intern

ONI PRESS, INC.
1305 SE Martin Luther King Jr. Blvd.
Suite A
Portland, OR 97214
USA

www.onipress.com
www.firstinspacecomic.com

First edition: April 2007
ISBN-13: 978-1-932664-64-5

1 3 5 7 9 10 8 6 4 2
PRINTED IN CANADA.

# Dedication

For my Father and Grandfathers

--Men of integrity who continue to teach me
my most important lessons.

"Ham performed his program outstandingly,
proving that man could survive the rigorous
and hazardous adventure of Space flight."

- Ed Dittmer

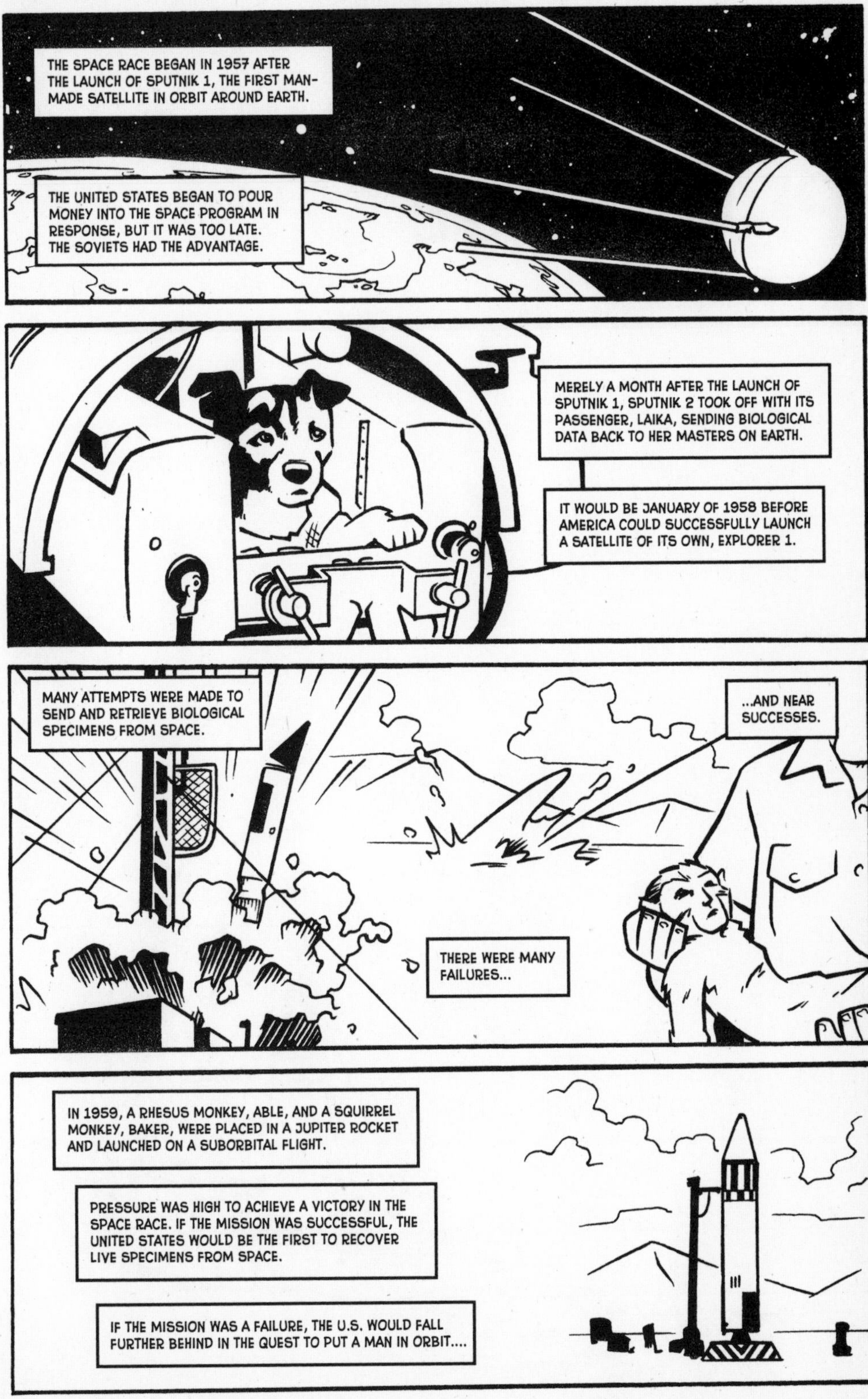
THE SPACE RACE BEGAN IN 1957 AFTER THE LAUNCH OF SPUTNIK 1, THE FIRST MAN-MADE SATELLITE IN ORBIT AROUND EARTH.
THE UNITED STATES BEGAN TO POUR MONEY INTO THE SPACE PROGRAM IN RESPONSE, BUT IT WAS TOO LATE. THE SOVIETS HAD THE ADVANTAGE.
MERELY A MONTH AFTER THE LAUNCH OF SPUTNIK 1, SPUTNIK 2 TOOK OFF WITH ITS PASSENGER, LAIKA, SENDING BIOLOGICAL DATA BACK TO HER MASTERS ON EARTH.
IT WOULD BE JANUARY OF 1958 BEFORE AMERICA COULD SUCCESSFULLY LAUNCH A SATELLITE OF ITS OWN, EXPLORER 1.
MANY ATTEMPTS WERE MADE TO SEND AND RETRIEVE BIOLOGICAL SPECIMENS FROM SPACE.
THERE WERE MANY FAILURES...
...AND NEAR SUCCESSES.
IN 1959, A RHESUS MONKEY, ABLE, AND A SQUIRREL MONKEY, BAKER, WERE PLACED IN A JUPITER ROCKET AND LAUNCHED ON A SUBORBITAL FLIGHT.
PRESSURE WAS HIGH TO ACHIEVE A VICTORY IN THE SPACE RACE. IF THE MISSION WAS SUCCESSFUL, THE UNITED STATES WOULD BE THE FIRST TO RECOVER LIVE SPECIMENS FROM SPACE.
IF THE MISSION WAS A FAILURE, THE U.S. WOULD FALL FURTHER BEHIND IN THE QUEST TO PUT A MAN IN ORBIT....

# PROLOGUE

MAY 28, 1959.

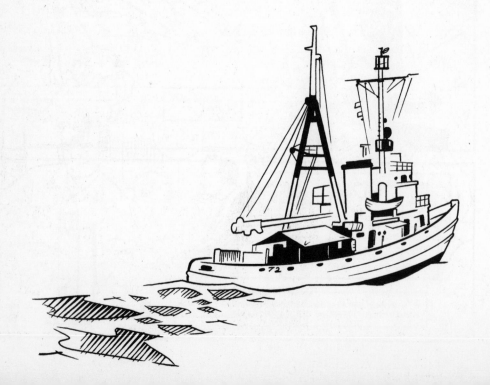

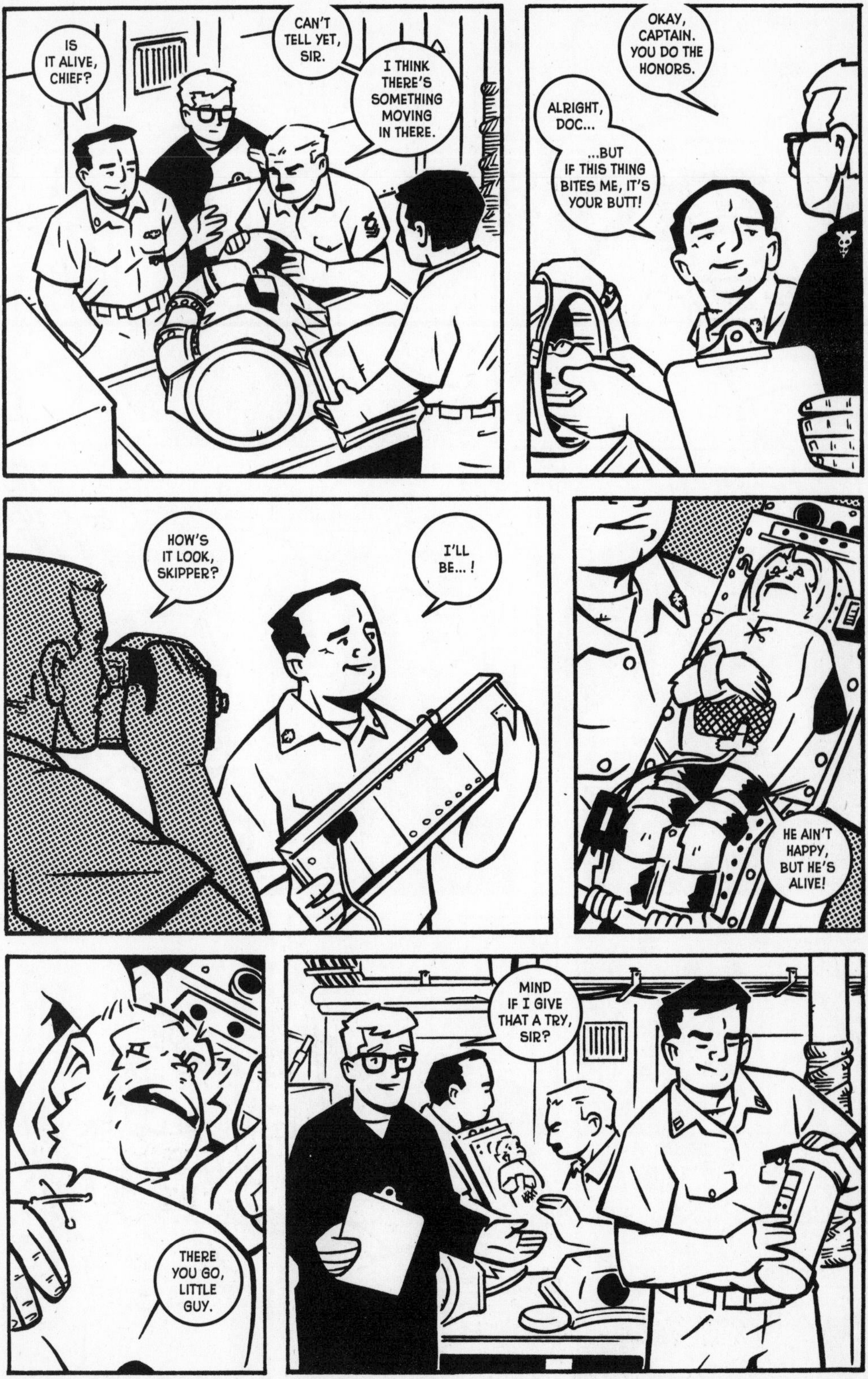
IS IT ALIVE, CHIEF?
CAN'T TELL YET, SIR.
I THINK THERE'S SOMETHING MOVING IN THERE.
OKAY, CAPTAIN. YOU DO THE HONORS.
ALRIGHT, DOC...
...BUT IF THIS THING BITES ME, IT'S YOUR BUTT!
HOW'S IT LOOK, SKIPPER?
I'LL BE... !
HE AIN'T HAPPY, BUT HE'S ALIVE!
THERE YOU GO, LITTLE GUY.
MIND IF I GIVE THAT A TRY, SIR?

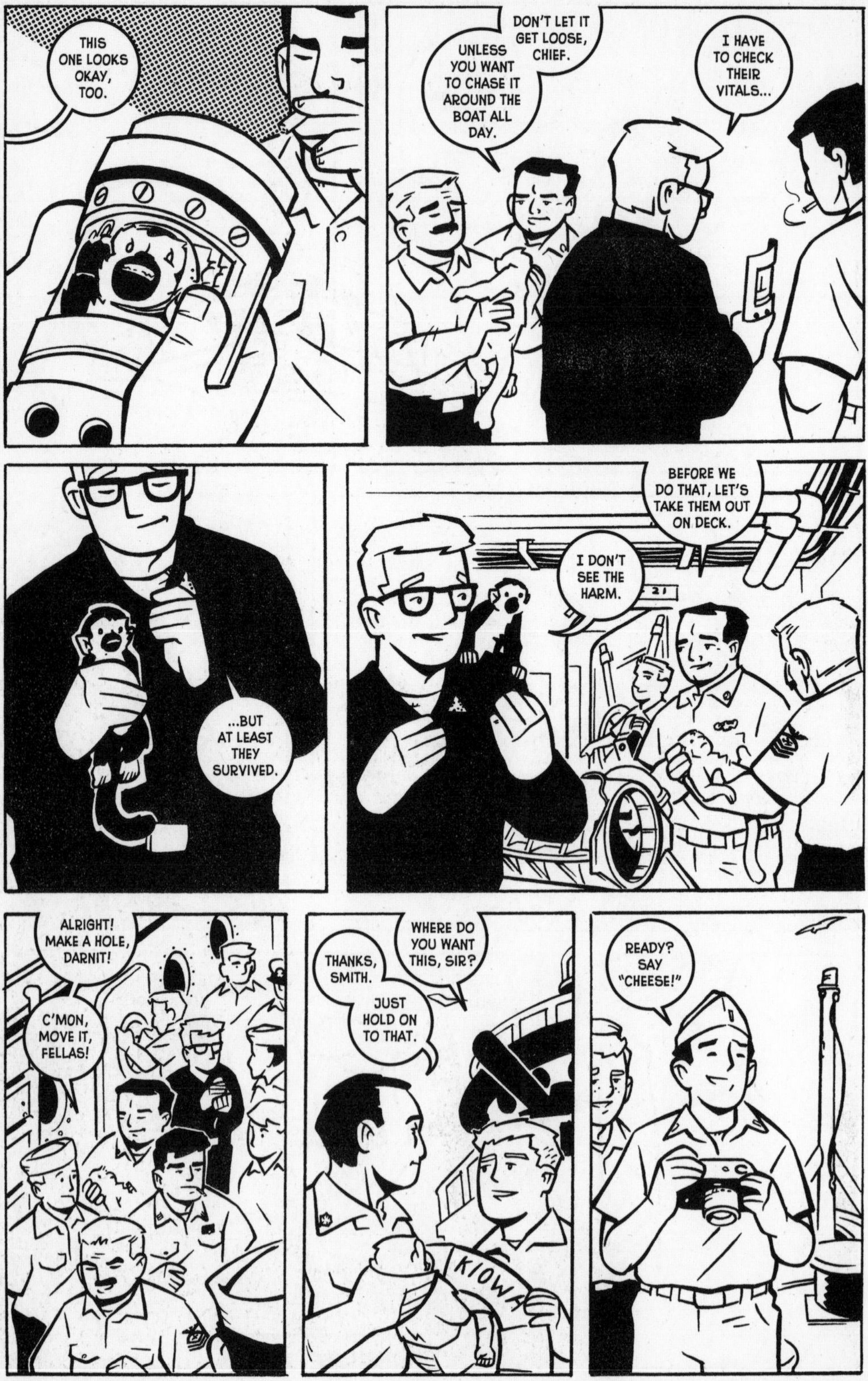
THIS ONE LOOKS OKAY, TOO.
DON'T LET IT GET LOOSE, CHIEF.
UNLESS YOU WANT TO CHASE IT AROUND THE BOAT ALL DAY.
I HAVE TO CHECK THEIR VITALS...
...BUT AT LEAST THEY SURVIVED.
BEFORE WE DO THAT, LET'S TAKE THEM OUT ON DECK.
I DON'T SEE THE HARM.
ALRIGHT! MAKE A HOLE, DARNIT!
C'MON, MOVE IT, FELLAS!
WHERE DO YOU WANT THIS, SIR?
THANKS, SMITH.
JUST HOLD ON TO THAT.
KIOWA
READY? SAY "CHEESE!"

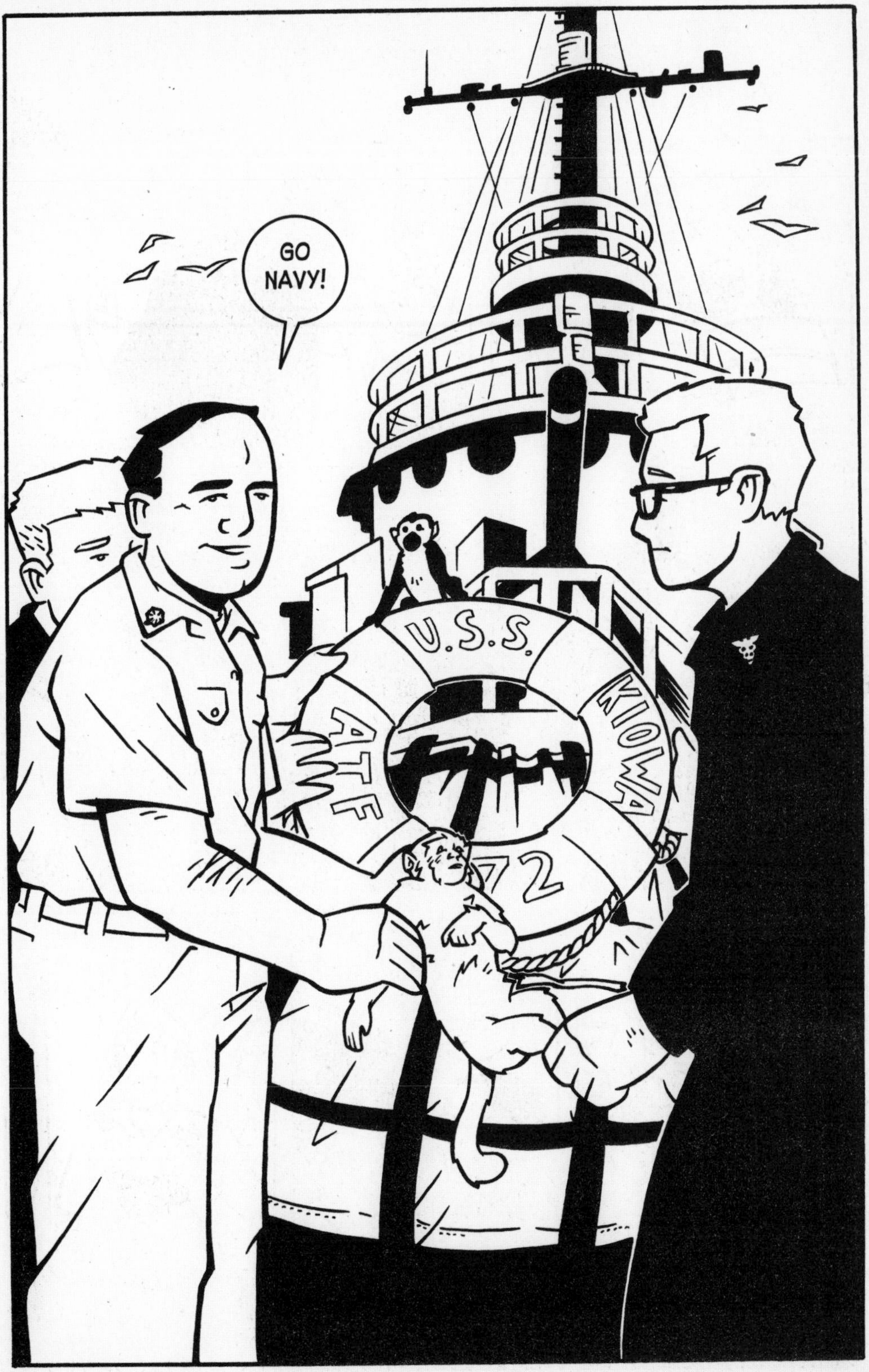
GO NAVY!
U.S.S.
KIOWA
ATF
72

# FIRST IN SPACE™

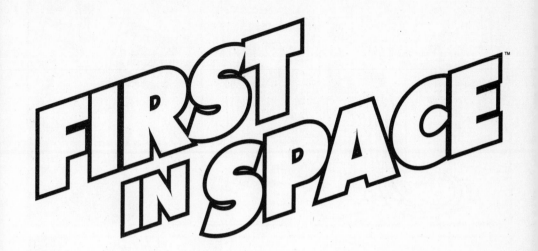

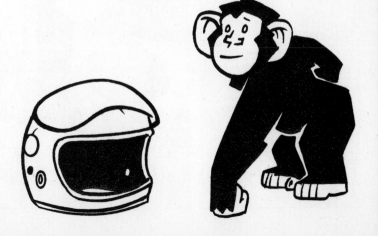

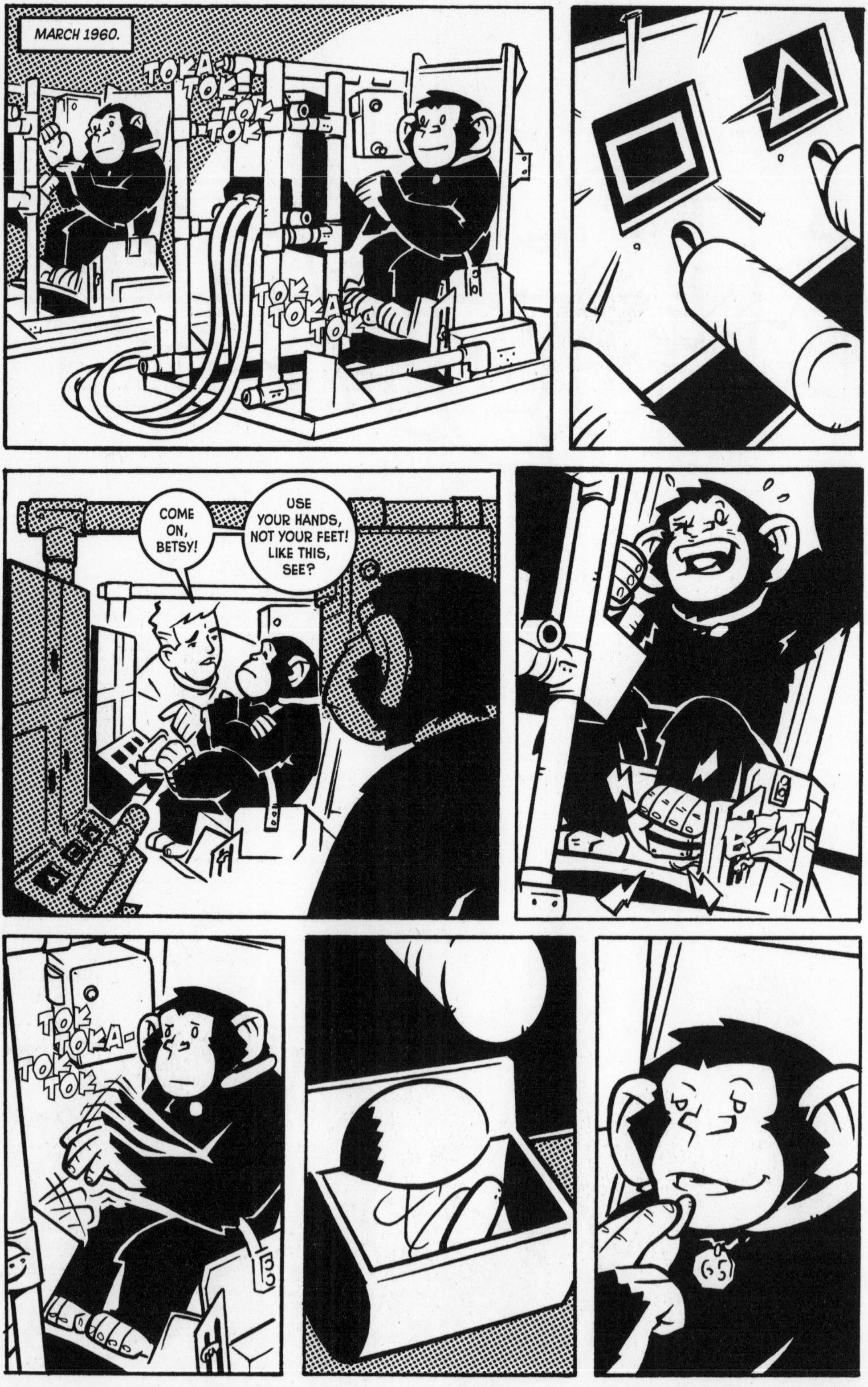
MARCH 1960.
TOKA-TOK-TOK-TOK
TOK TOKA-TOK
COME ON, BETSY!
USE YOUR HANDS, NOT YOUR FEET! LIKE THIS, SEE?
BZT
TOK TOKA-TOK TOK
65

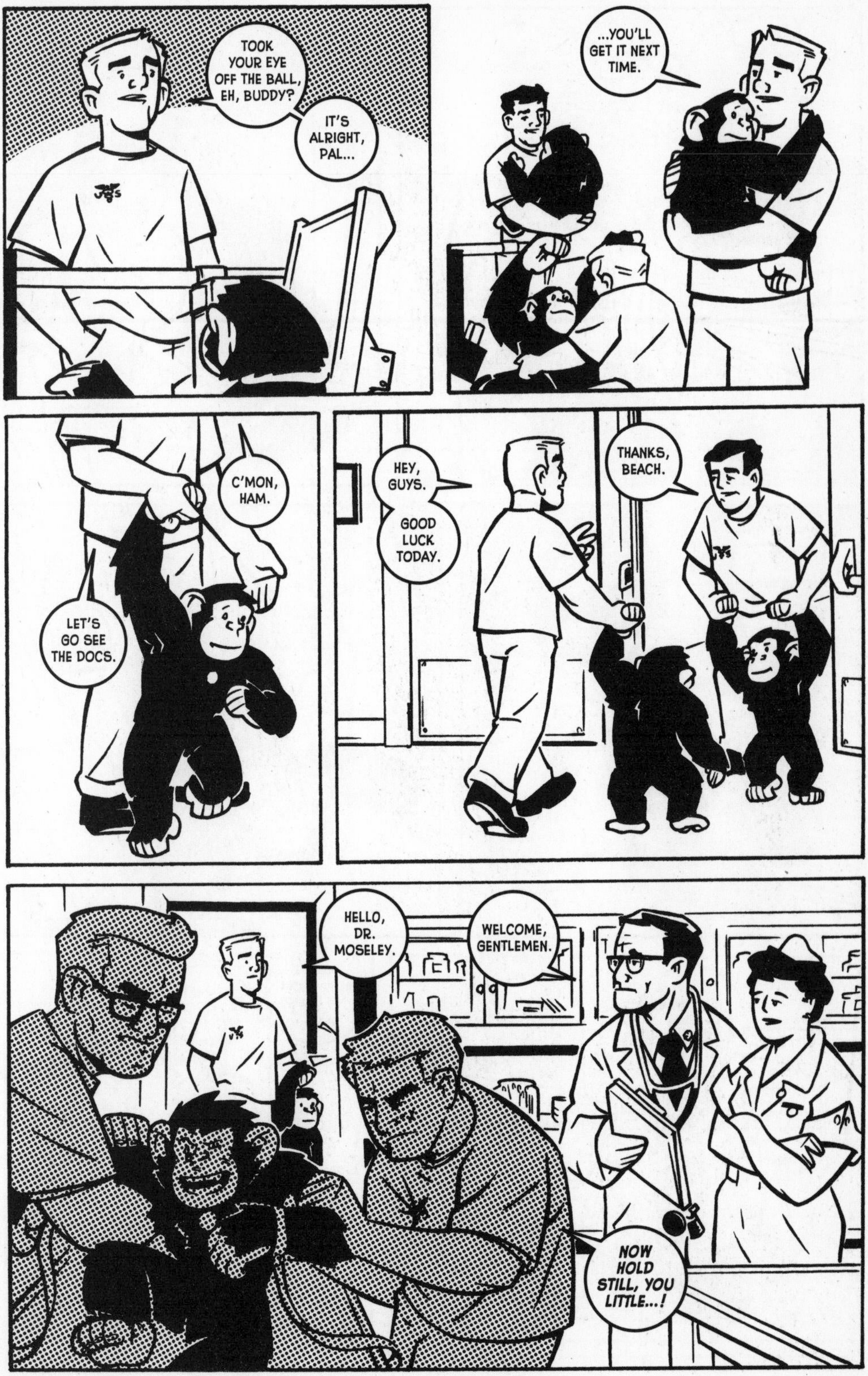
TOOK YOUR EYE OFF THE BALL, EH, BUDDY?
IT'S ALRIGHT, PAL...
...YOU'LL GET IT NEXT TIME.
C'MON, HAM.
LET'S GO SEE THE DOCS.
HEY, GUYS.
GOOD LUCK TODAY.
THANKS, BEACH.
HELLO, DR. MOSELEY.
WELCOME, GENTLEMEN.
NOW HOLD STILL, YOU LITTLE...!

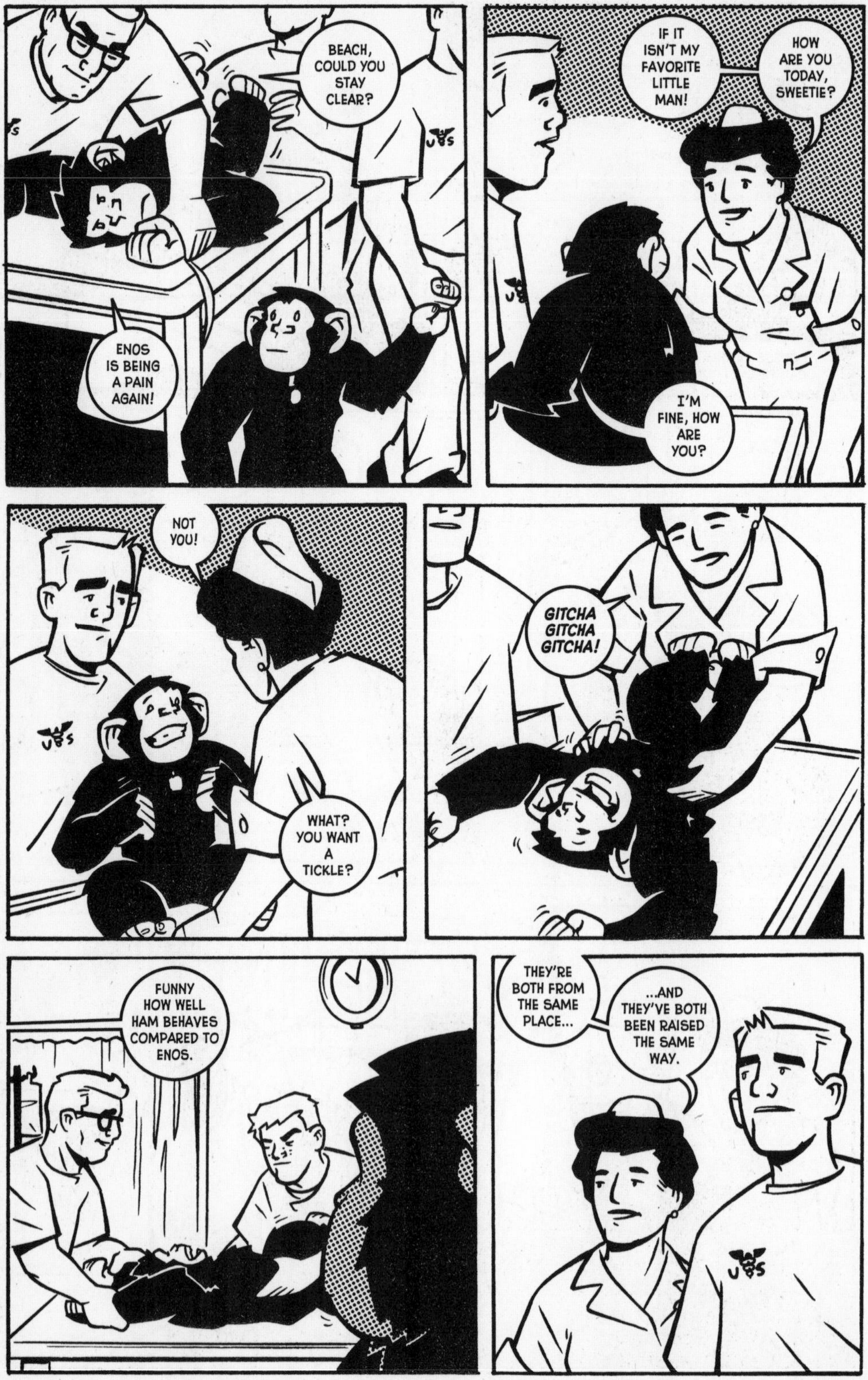
BEACH, COULD YOU STAY CLEAR?
ENOS IS BEING A PAIN AGAIN!
IF IT ISN'T MY FAVORITE LITTLE MAN!
HOW ARE YOU TODAY, SWEETIE?
I'M FINE, HOW ARE YOU?
NOT YOU!
WHAT? YOU WANT A TICKLE?
GITCHA GITCHA GITCHA!
FUNNY HOW WELL HAM BEHAVES COMPARED TO ENOS.
THEY'RE BOTH FROM THE SAME PLACE...
...AND THEY'VE BOTH BEEN RAISED THE SAME WAY.

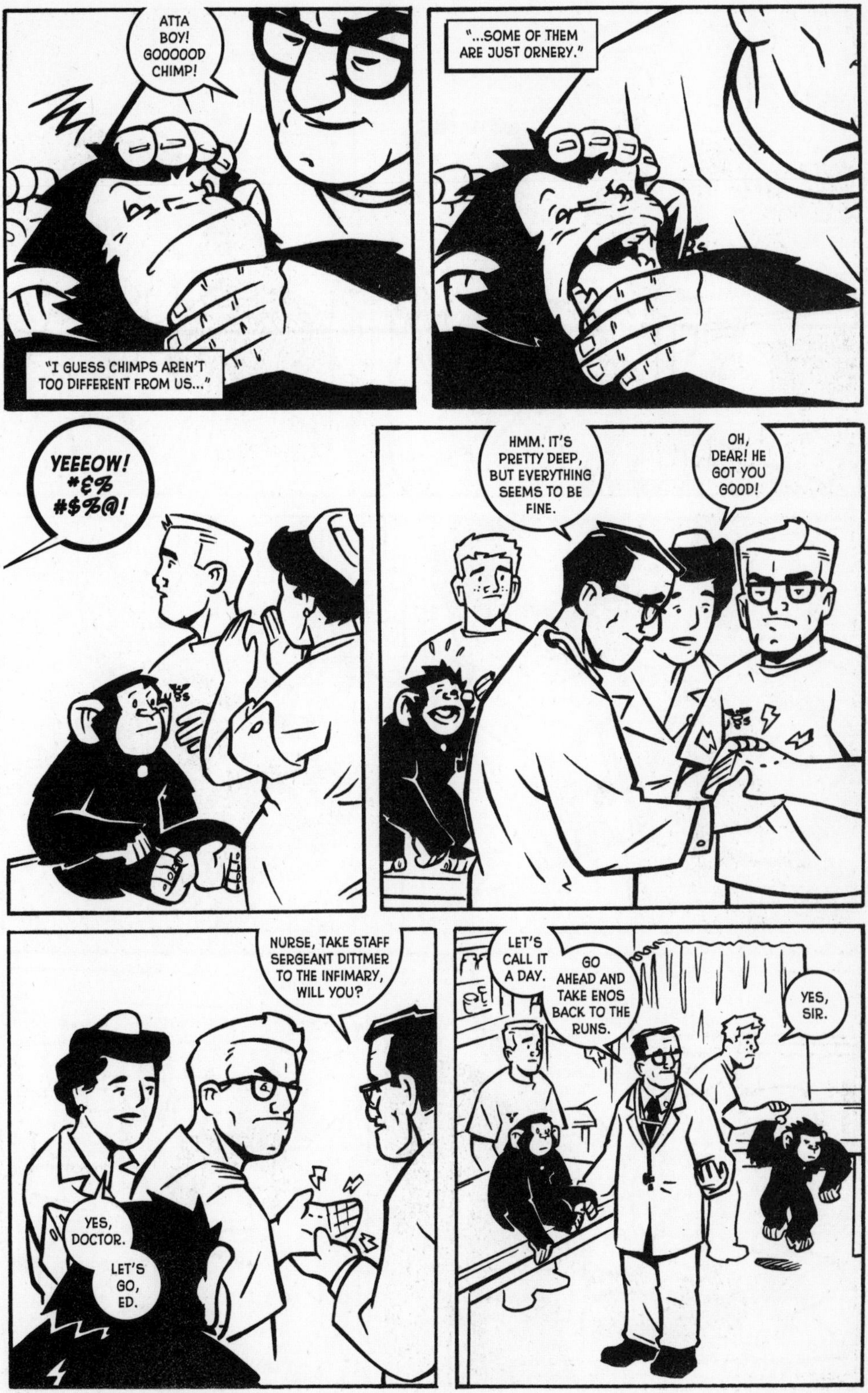
ATTA BOY! GOOOOOD CHIMP!
"I GUESS CHIMPS AREN'T TOO DIFFERENT FROM US..."
"...SOME OF THEM ARE JUST ORNERY."
YEEEOW! #&% #$%@!
HMM. IT'S PRETTY DEEP, BUT EVERYTHING SEEMS TO BE FINE.
OH, DEAR! HE GOT YOU GOOD!
NURSE, TAKE STAFF SERGEANT DITTMER TO THE INFIMARY, WILL YOU?
YES, DOCTOR.
LET'S GO, ED.
LET'S CALL IT A DAY.
GO AHEAD AND TAKE ENOS BACK TO THE RUNS.
YES, SIR.

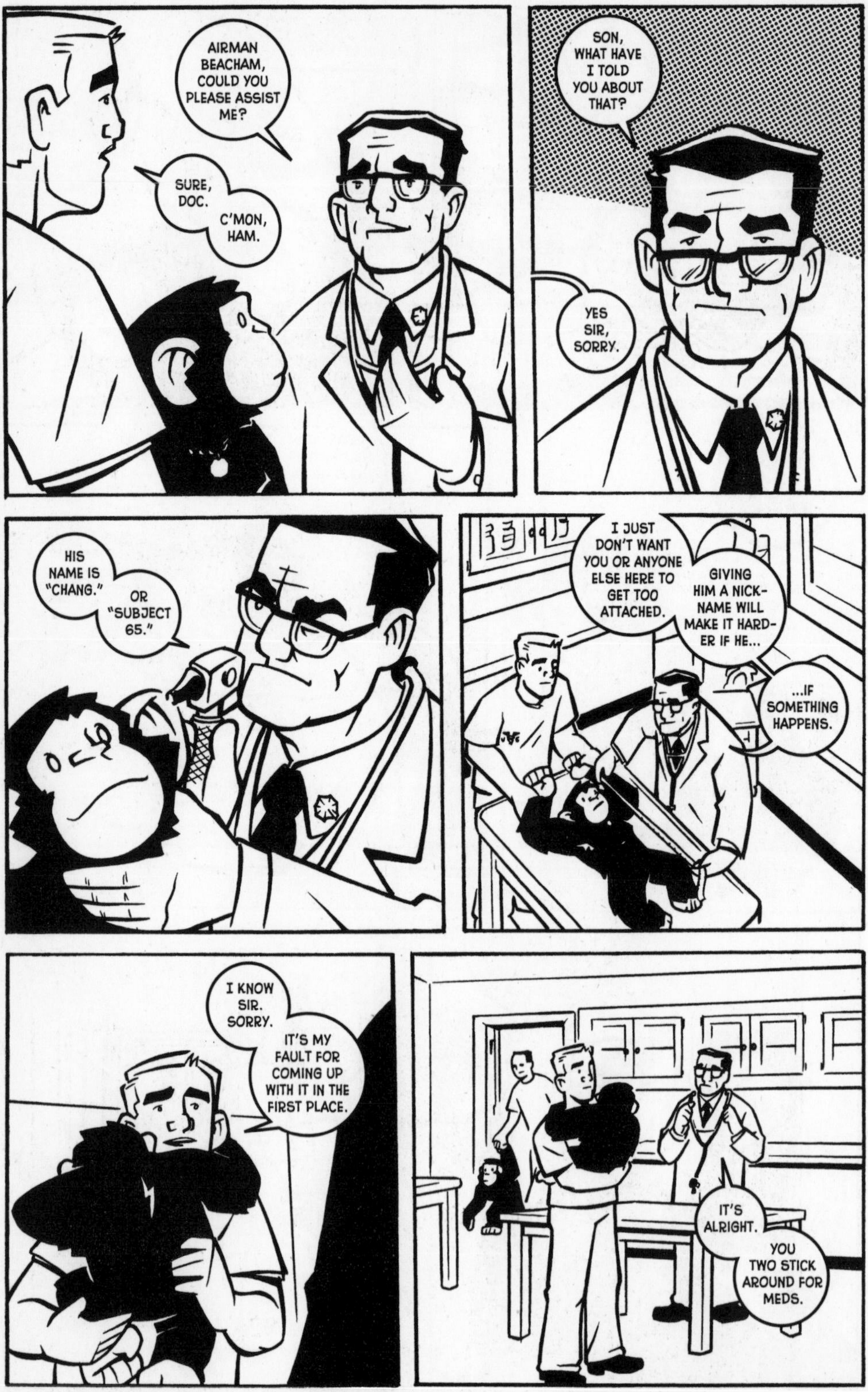
AIRMAN BEACHAM, COULD YOU PLEASE ASSIST ME?
SURE, DOC.
C'MON, HAM.
SON, WHAT HAVE I TOLD YOU ABOUT THAT?
YES SIR, SORRY.
HIS NAME IS "CHANG."
OR "SUBJECT 65."
I JUST DON'T WANT YOU OR ANYONE ELSE HERE TO GET TOO ATTACHED.
GIVING HIM A NICK-NAME WILL MAKE IT HARDER IF HE...
...IF SOMETHING HAPPENS.
I KNOW SIR. SORRY.
IT'S MY FAULT FOR COMING UP WITH IT IN THE FIRST PLACE.
IT'S ALRIGHT.
YOU TWO STICK AROUND FOR MEDS.

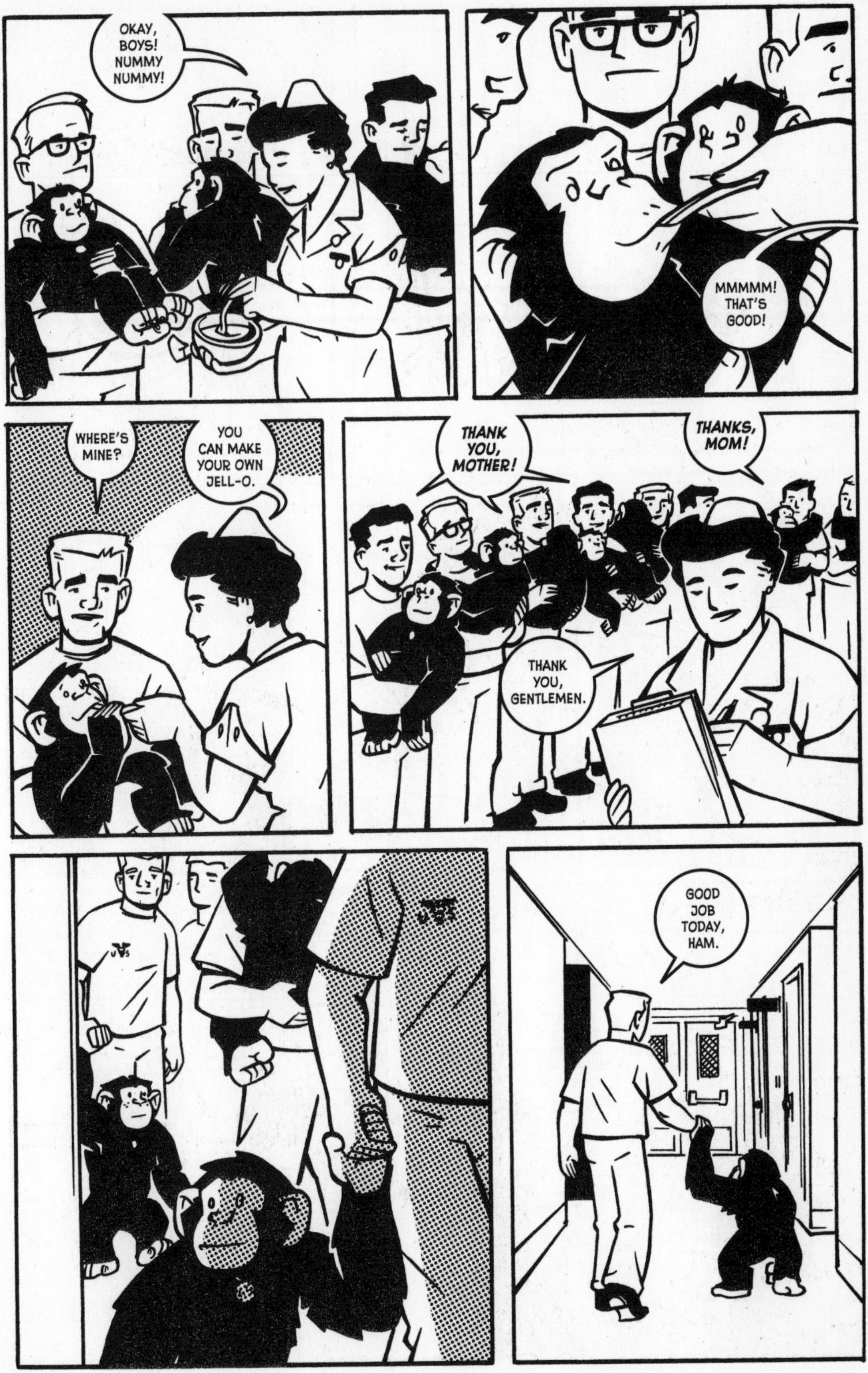
OKAY, BOYS! NUMMY NUMMY!
MMMMM! THAT'S GOOD!
WHERE'S MINE?
YOU CAN MAKE YOUR OWN JELL-O.
THANK YOU, MOTHER!
THANKS, MOM!
THANK YOU, GENTLEMEN.
GOOD JOB TODAY, HAM.

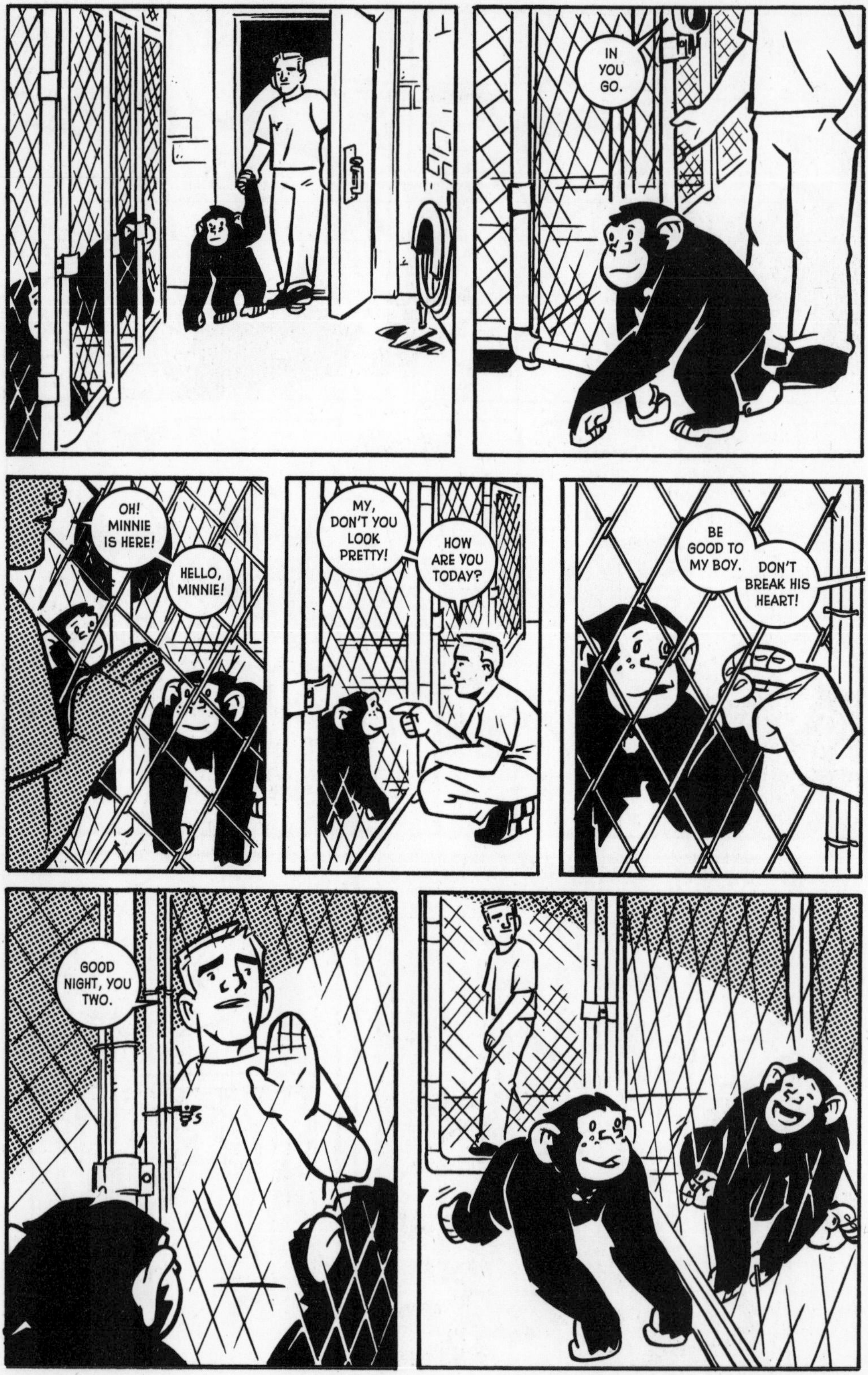
IN YOU GO.
OH! MINNIE IS HERE!
HELLO, MINNIE!
MY, DON'T YOU LOOK PRETTY!
HOW ARE YOU TODAY?
BE GOOD TO MY BOY.
DON'T BREAK HIS HEART!
GOOD NIGHT, YOU TWO.

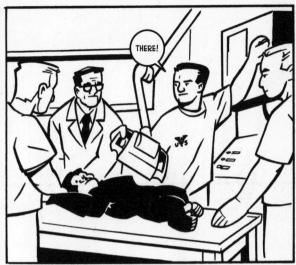

**THERE!**

HOLD STILL, LITTLE GUY. THIS WILL... ...TAKE... ...A SECOND.

GET THOSE DEVELOPED AS SOON AS YOU CAN, PLEASE.

YES, DR. FINEG.

I'M CONCERNED THAT 65 MIGHT BE GROWING TOO FAST. SEE HERE?

HE DOES SEEM TO BE GETTING PRETTY BIG.

YOU, MY HAIRY LITTLE FRIEND, ARE GETTING TOO BIG FOR YOUR BRITCHES!

WHAT DOES THAT MEAN, SIR?

IT MEANS THAT IF HE KEEPS GROWING LIKE THIS, CHANG IS GOING TO QUICKLY EXCEED OUR WEIGHT LIMITS.

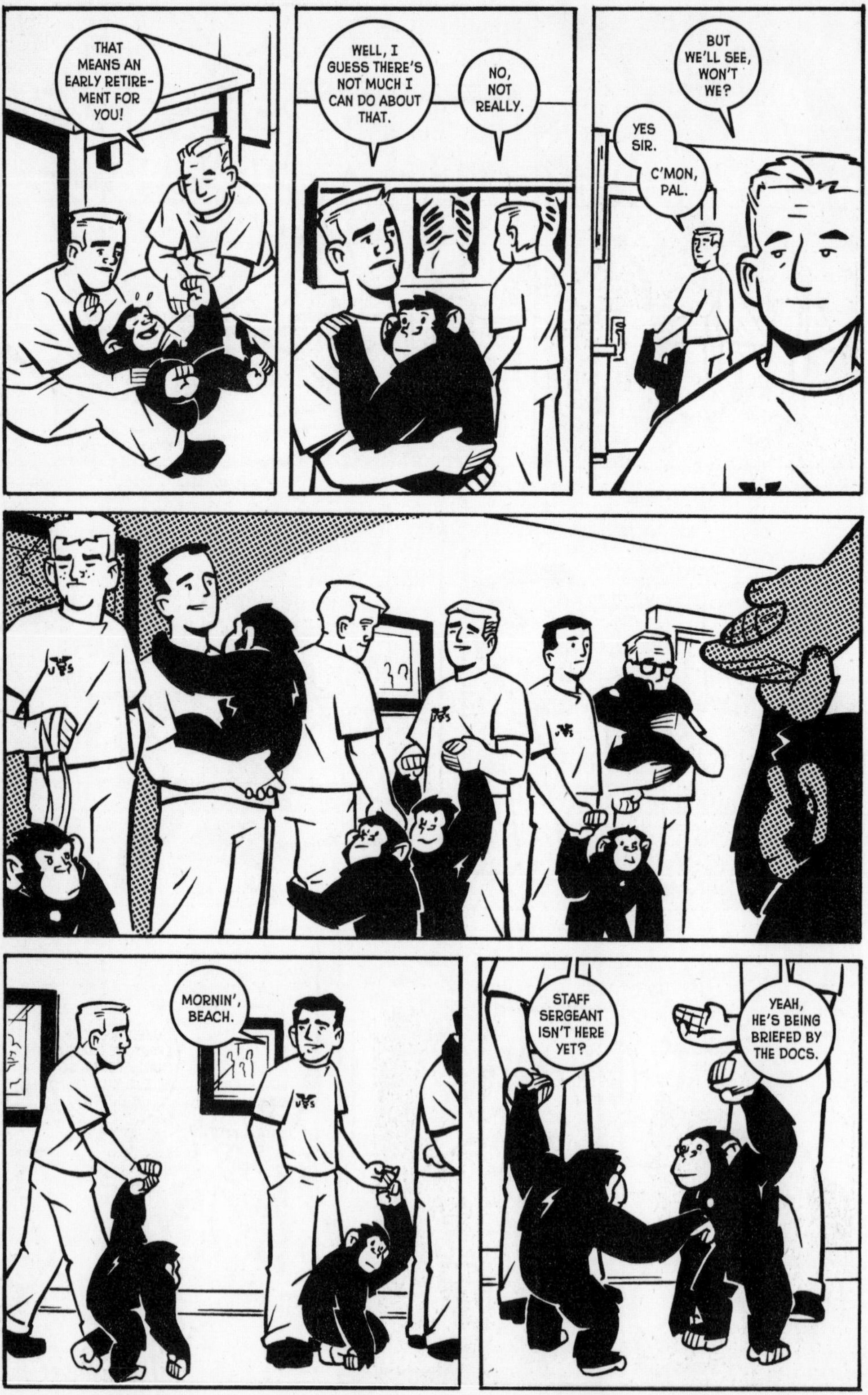
THAT MEANS AN EARLY RETIRE-MENT FOR YOU!
WELL, I GUESS THERE'S NOT MUCH I CAN DO ABOUT THAT.
NO, NOT REALLY.
BUT WE'LL SEE, WON'T WE?
YES SIR.
C'MON, PAL.
MORNIN', BEACH.
STAFF SERGEANT ISN'T HERE YET?
YEAH, HE'S BEING BRIEFED BY THE DOCS.

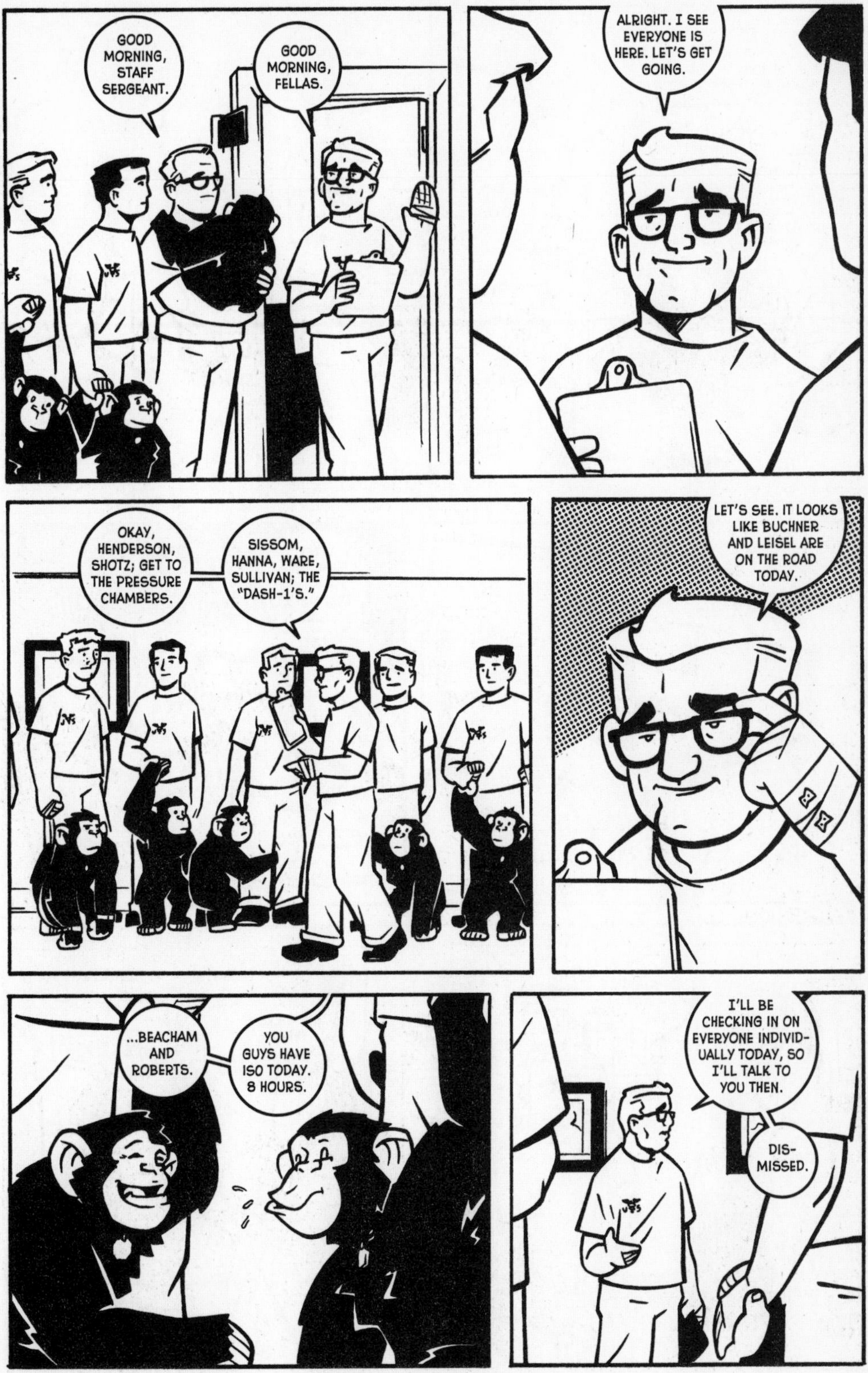
GOOD MORNING, STAFF SERGEANT.
GOOD MORNING, FELLAS.
ALRIGHT. I SEE EVERYONE IS HERE. LET'S GET GOING.
OKAY, HENDERSON, SHOTZ; GET TO THE PRESSURE CHAMBERS.
SISSOM, HANNA, WARE, SULLIVAN; THE "DASH-1'S."
LET'S SEE. IT LOOKS LIKE BUCHNER AND LEISEL ARE ON THE ROAD TODAY.
...BEACHAM AND ROBERTS.
YOU GUYS HAVE ISO TODAY. 8 HOURS.
I'LL BE CHECKING IN ON EVERYONE INDIVIDUALLY TODAY, SO I'LL TALK TO YOU THEN.
DIS-MISSED.

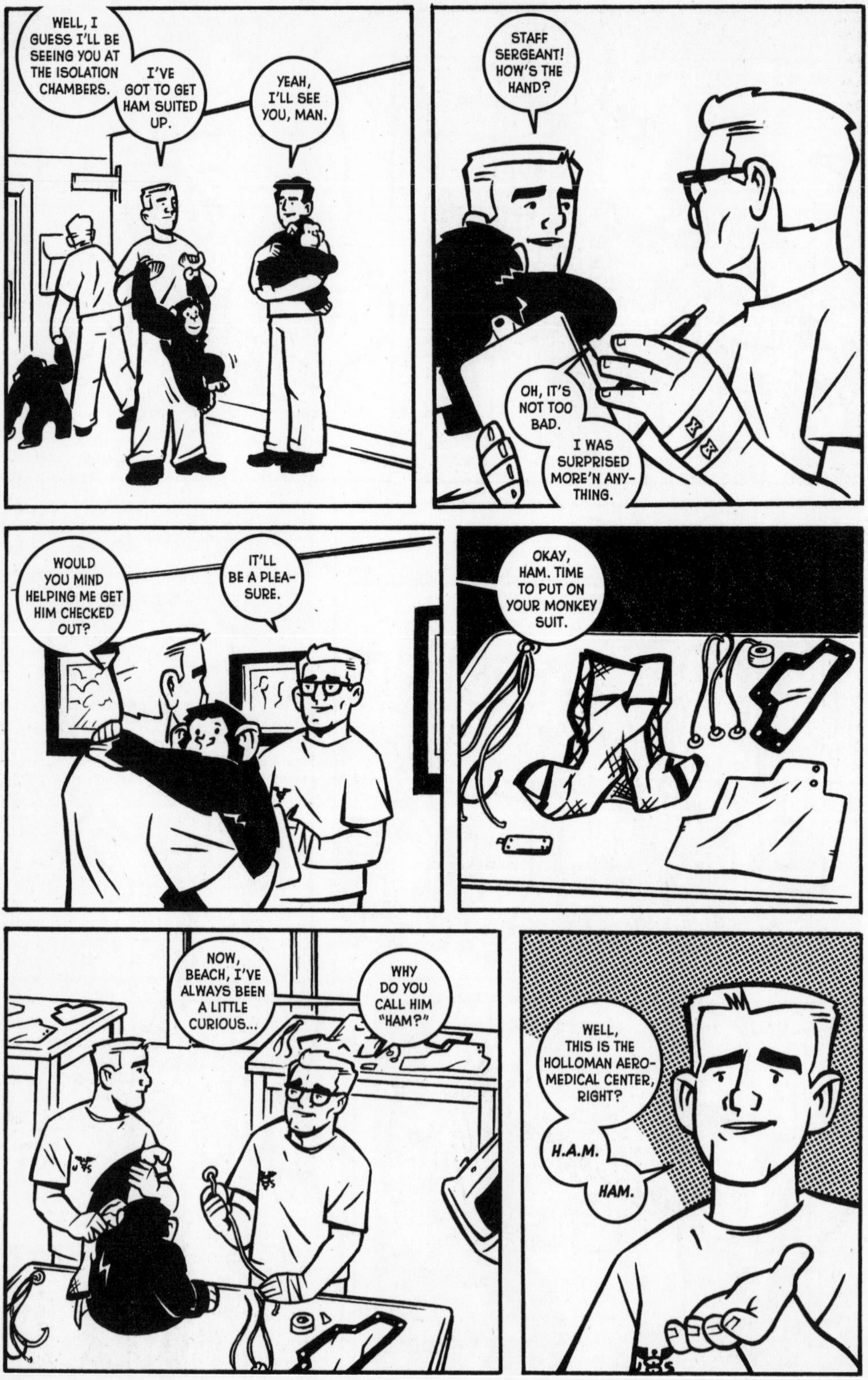
WELL, I GUESS I'LL BE SEEING YOU AT THE ISOLATION CHAMBERS.
I'VE GOT TO GET HAM SUITED UP.
YEAH, I'LL SEE YOU, MAN.
STAFF SERGEANT! HOW'S THE HAND?
OH, IT'S NOT TOO BAD.
I WAS SURPRISED MORE'N ANYTHING.
WOULD YOU MIND HELPING ME GET HIM CHECKED OUT?
IT'LL BE A PLEASURE.
OKAY, HAM. TIME TO PUT ON YOUR MONKEY SUIT.
NOW, BEACH, I'VE ALWAYS BEEN A LITTLE CURIOUS...
WHY DO YOU CALL HIM "HAM?"
WELL, THIS IS THE HOLLOMAN AERO-MEDICAL CENTER, RIGHT?
H.A.M.
HAM.

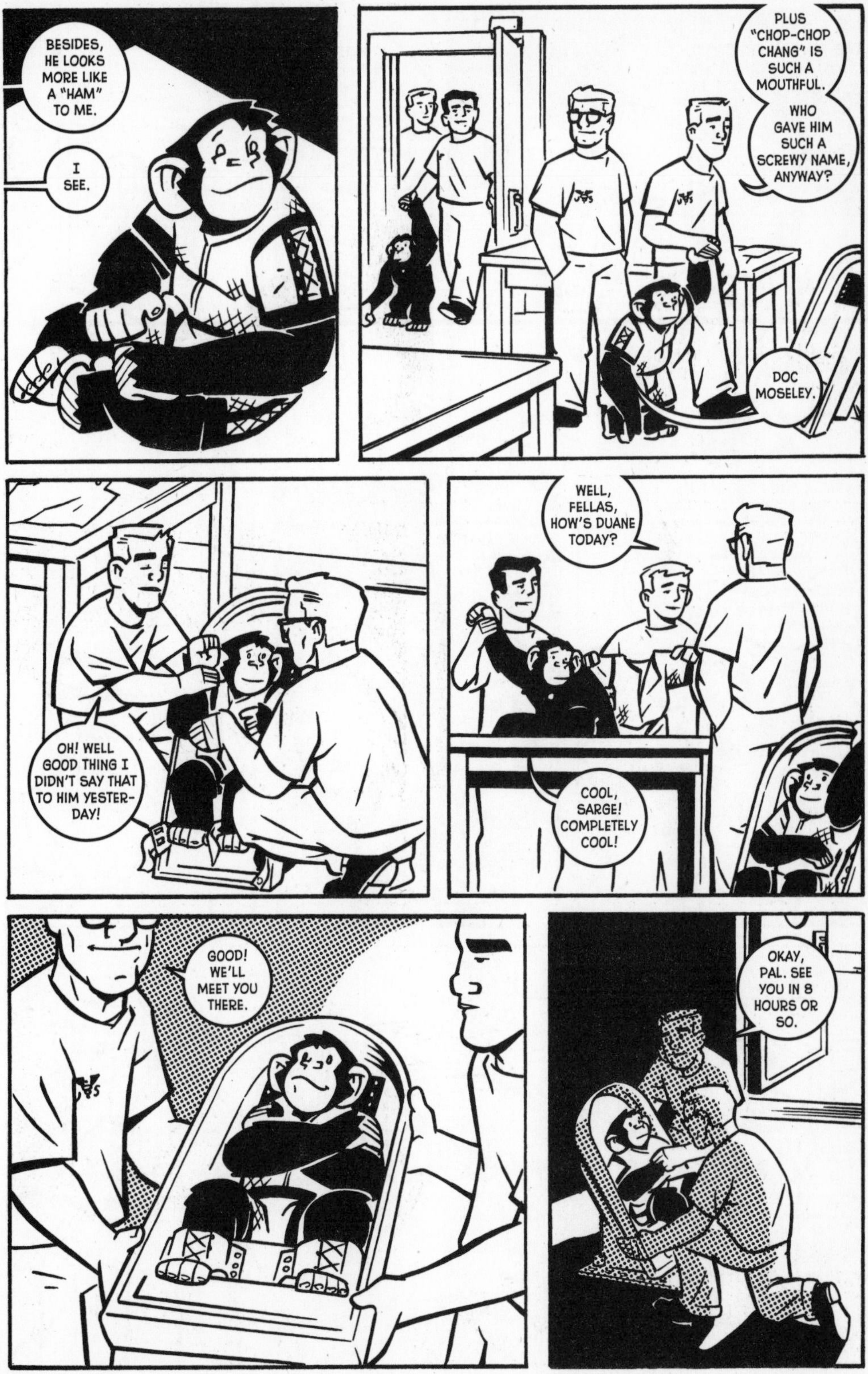
BESIDES, HE LOOKS MORE LIKE A "HAM" TO ME.
I SEE.
PLUS "CHOP-CHOP CHANG" IS SUCH A MOUTHFUL.
WHO GAVE HIM SUCH A SCREWY NAME, ANYWAY?
DOC MOSELEY.
OH! WELL GOOD THING I DIDN'T SAY THAT TO HIM YESTER-DAY!
WELL, FELLAS, HOW'S DUANE TODAY?
COOL, SARGE! COMPLETELY COOL!
GOOD! WE'LL MEET YOU THERE.
OKAY, PAL. SEE YOU IN 8 HOURS OR SO.

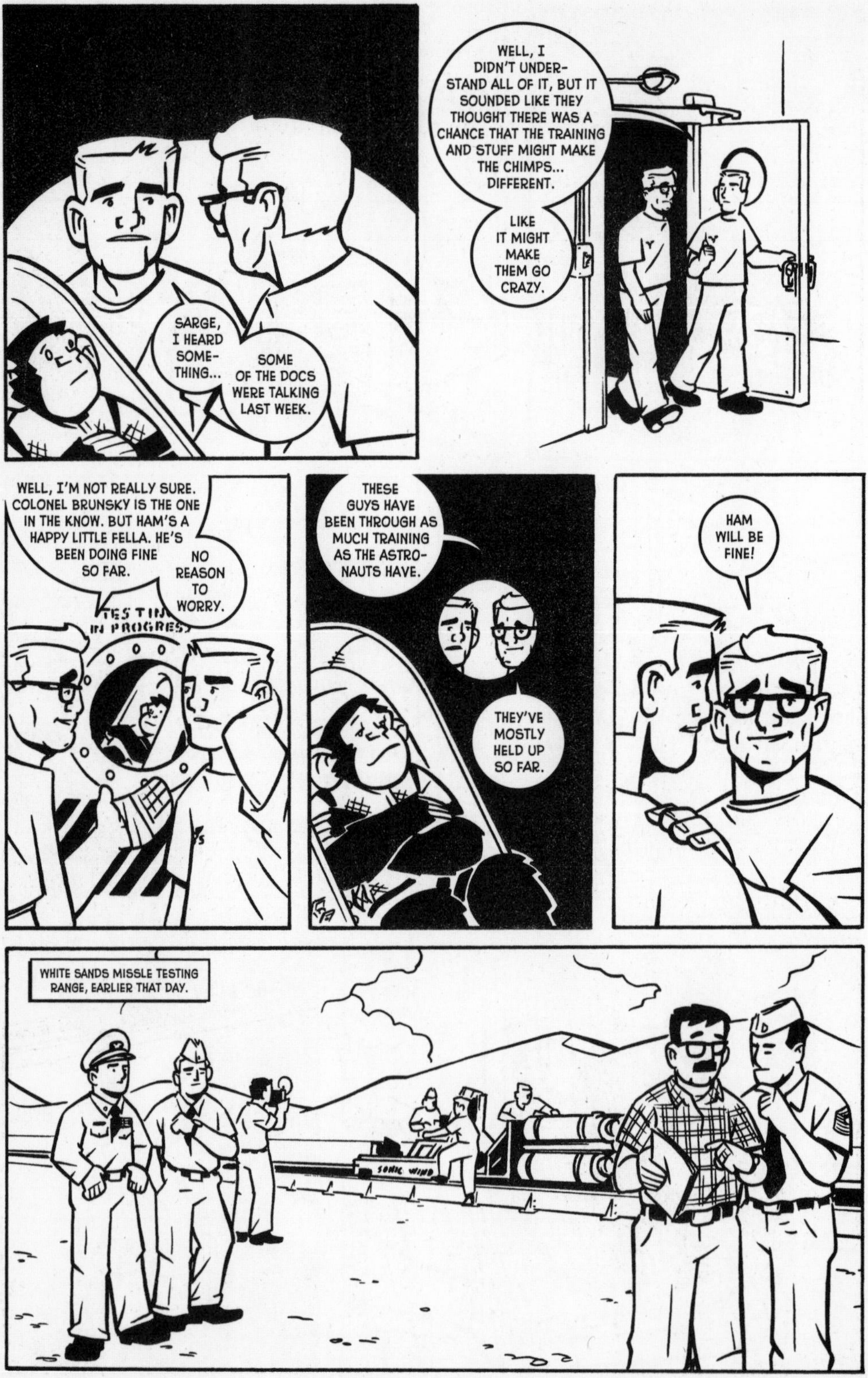
SARGE, I HEARD SOME-THING...
SOME OF THE DOCS WERE TALKING LAST WEEK.
WELL, I DIDN'T UNDER-STAND ALL OF IT, BUT IT SOUNDED LIKE THEY THOUGHT THERE WAS A CHANCE THAT THE TRAINING AND STUFF MIGHT MAKE THE CHIMPS... DIFFERENT.
LIKE IT MIGHT MAKE THEM GO CRAZY.
WELL, I'M NOT REALLY SURE. COLONEL BRUNSKY IS THE ONE IN THE KNOW. BUT HAM'S A HAPPY LITTLE FELLA. HE'S BEEN DOING FINE SO FAR.
NO REASON TO WORRY.
IN PROGRESS
THESE GUYS HAVE BEEN THROUGH AS MUCH TRAINING AS THE ASTRO-NAUTS HAVE.
THEY'VE MOSTLY HELD UP SO FAR.
HAM WILL BE FINE!
WHITE SANDS MISSLE TESTING RANGE, EARLIER THAT DAY.
SONIC WIND

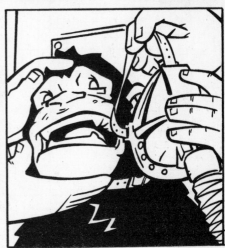

ALL PERSONNEL DOWNRANGE!

T-MINUS 3... 2...

DANGER

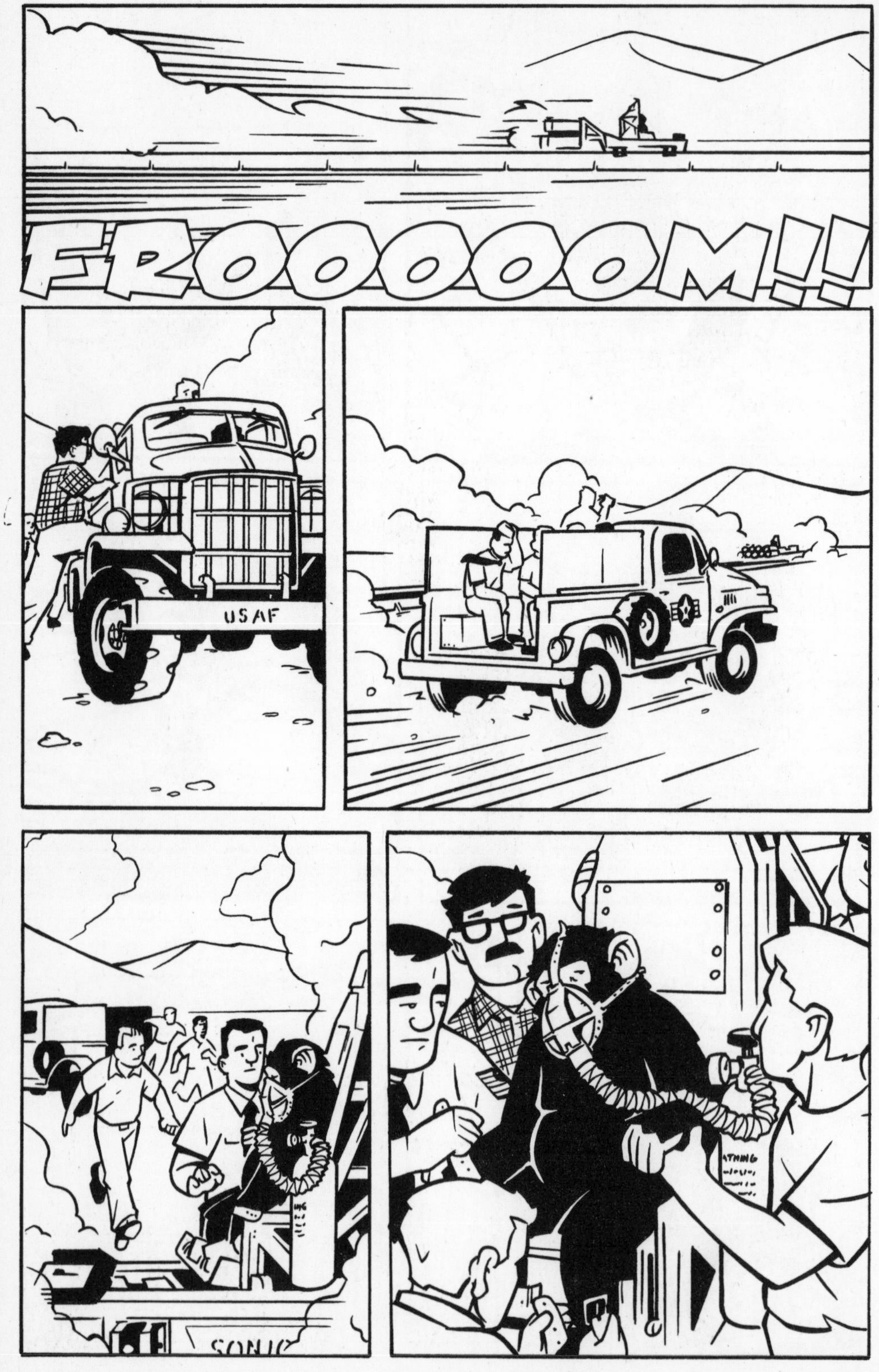
FROOOOOM!!
USAF
SONIC

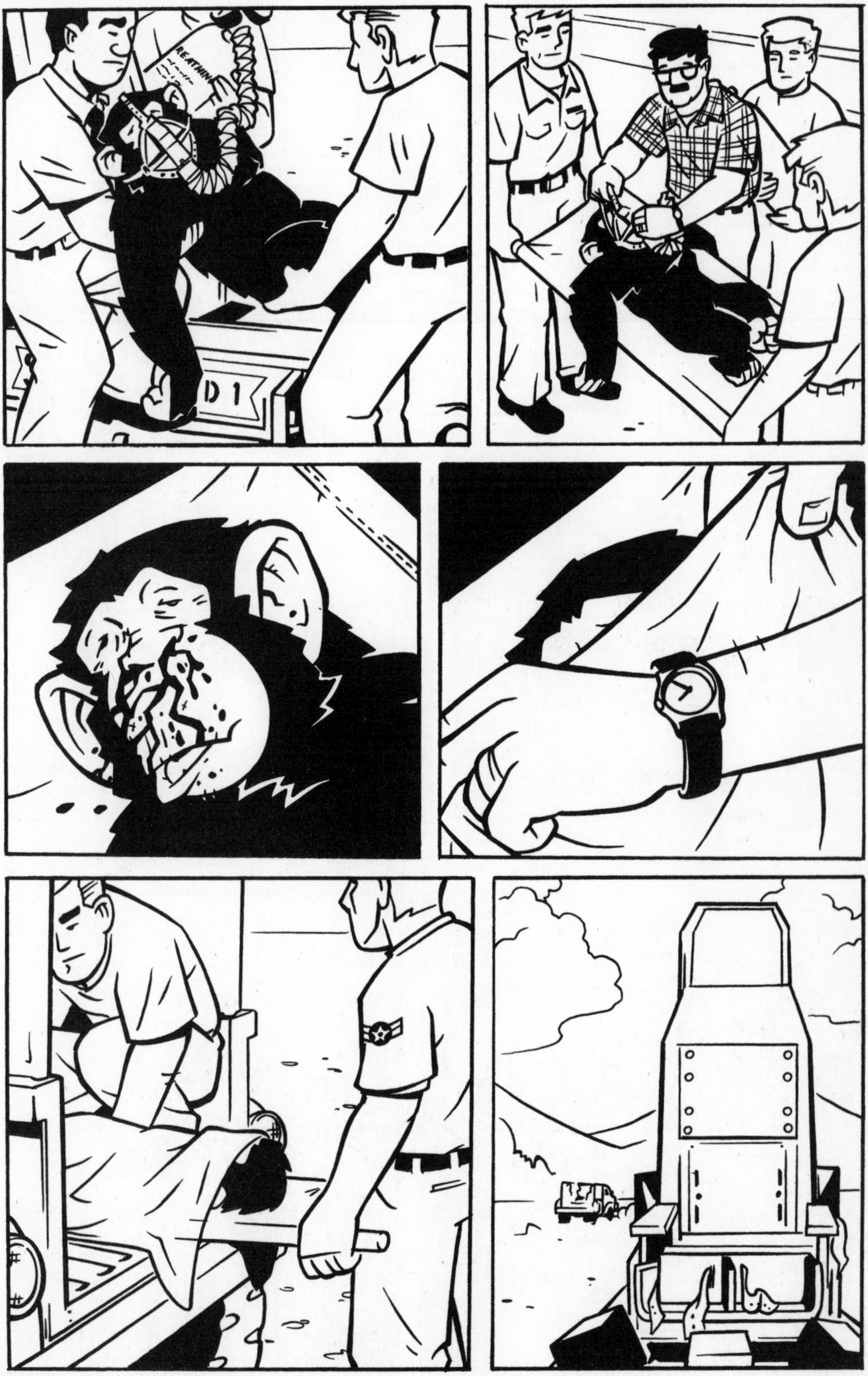
D1

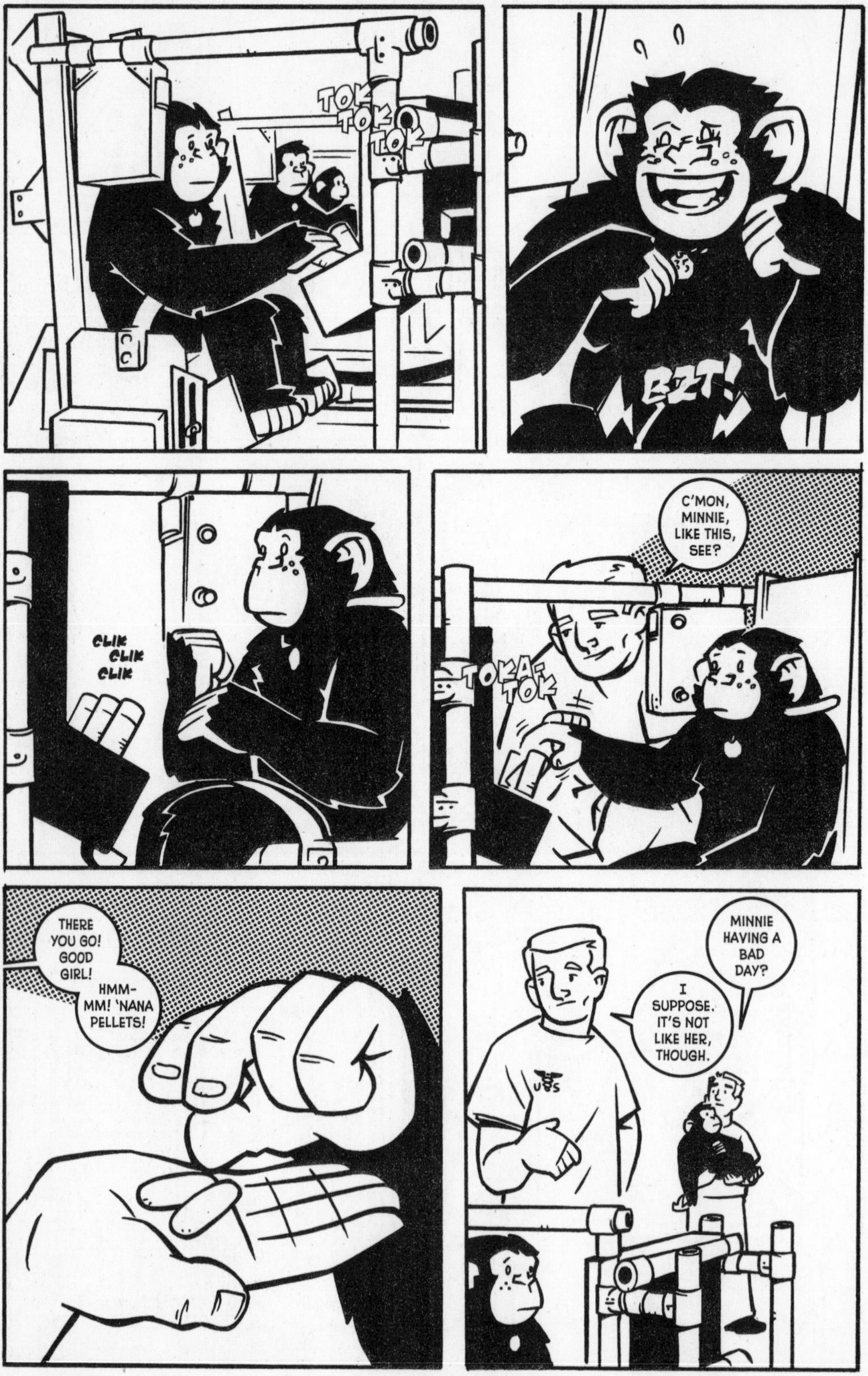
TOK
TOK
TOK
BZT!
CLIK
CLIK
CLIK
C'MON, MINNIE, LIKE THIS, SEE?
TOKA-TOK
THERE YOU GO! GOOD GIRL!
HMM-MM! 'NANA PELLETS!
MINNIE HAVING A BAD DAY?
I SUPPOSE. IT'S NOT LIKE HER, THOUGH.

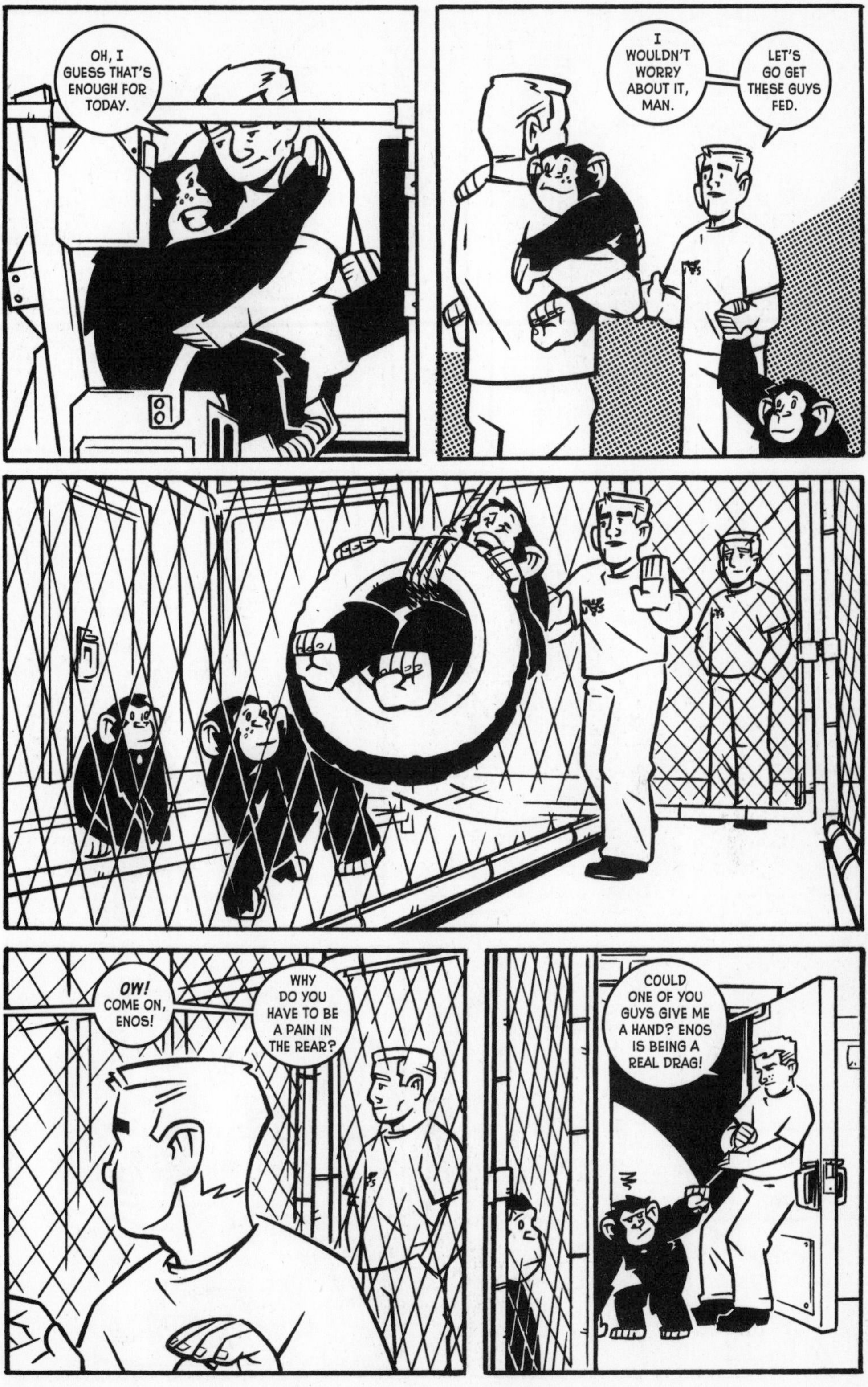
OH, I GUESS THAT'S ENOUGH FOR TODAY.
I WOULDN'T WORRY ABOUT IT, MAN.
LET'S GO GET THESE GUYS FED.
OW! COME ON, ENOS!
WHY DO YOU HAVE TO BE A PAIN IN THE REAR?
COULD ONE OF YOU GUYS GIVE ME A HAND? ENOS IS BEING A REAL DRAG!

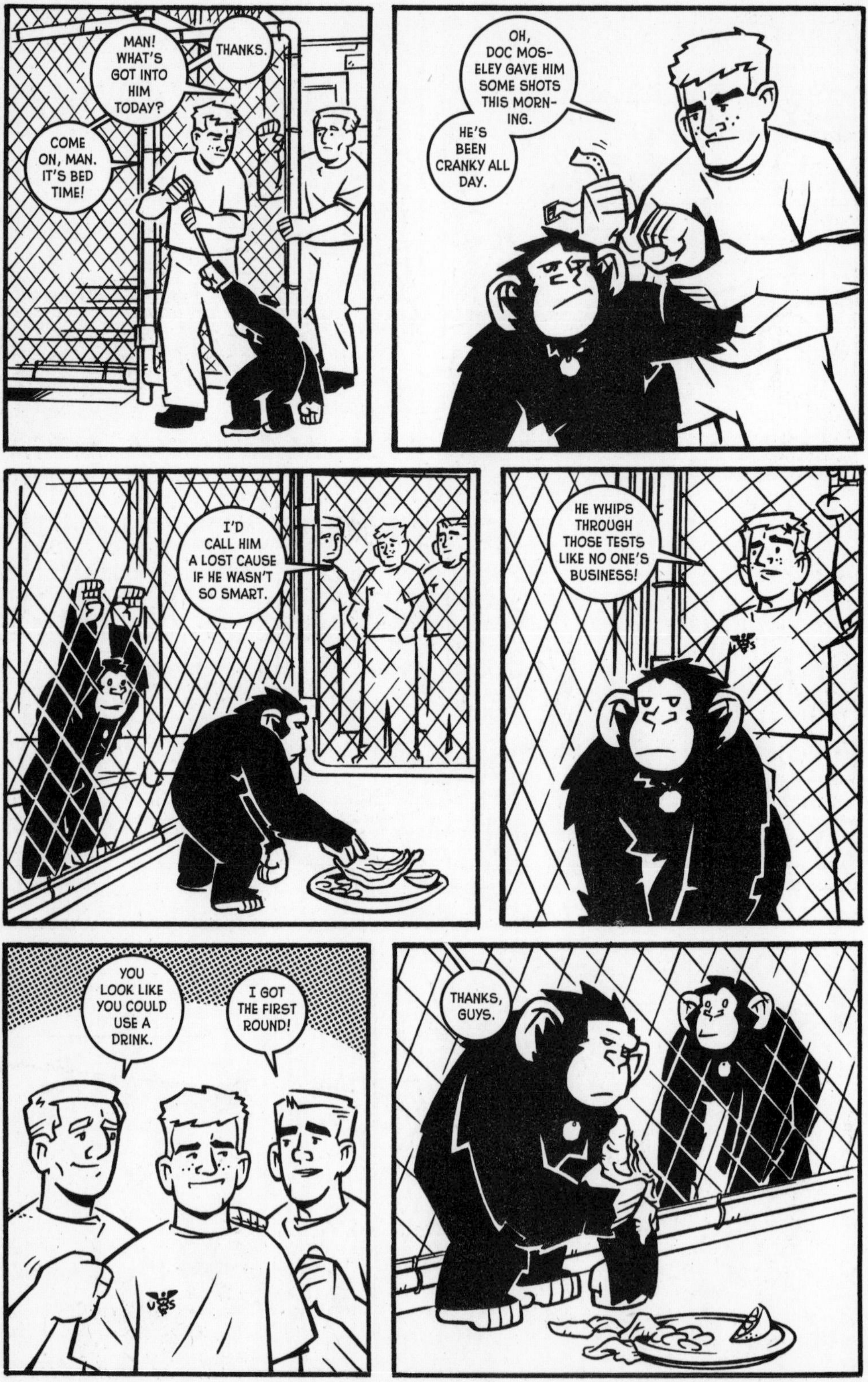
MAN! WHAT'S GOT INTO HIM TODAY?
THANKS.
COME ON, MAN. IT'S BED TIME!
OH, DOC MOSELEY GAVE HIM SOME SHOTS THIS MORNING.
HE'S BEEN CRANKY ALL DAY.
I'D CALL HIM A LOST CAUSE IF HE WASN'T SO SMART.
HE WHIPS THROUGH THOSE TESTS LIKE NO ONE'S BUSINESS!
YOU LOOK LIKE YOU COULD USE A DRINK.
I GOT THE FIRST ROUND!
THANKS, GUYS.

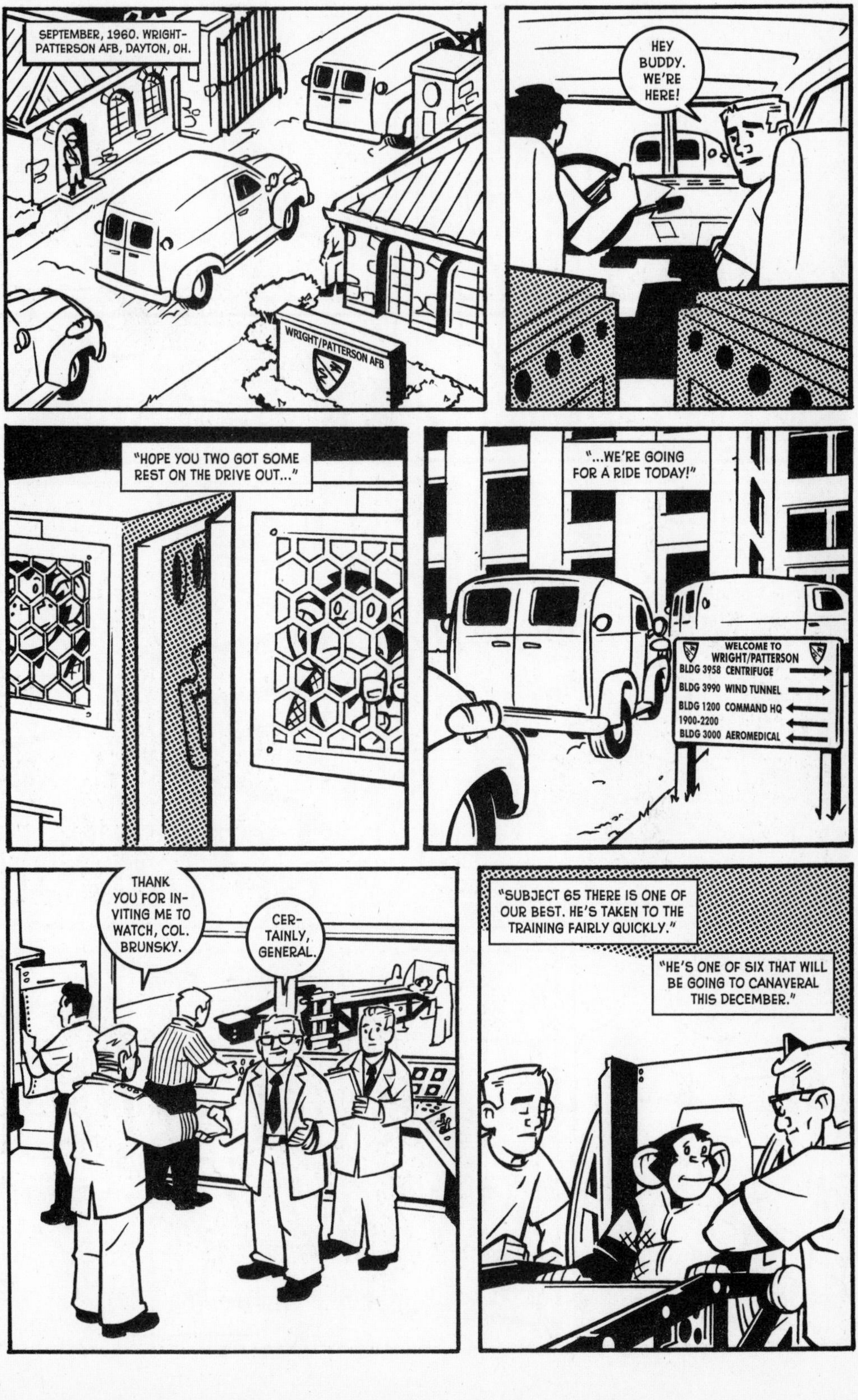
SEPTEMBER, 1960. WRIGHT-PATTERSON AFB, DAYTON, OH.
WRIGHT/PATTERSON AFB
HEY BUDDY. WE'RE HERE!
"HOPE YOU TWO GOT SOME REST ON THE DRIVE OUT..."
"...WE'RE GOING FOR A RIDE TODAY!"
WELCOME TO WRIGHT/PATTERSON
BLDG 3958 CENTRIFUGE
BLDG 3990 WIND TUNNEL
BLDG 1200 COMMAND HQ
1900-2200
BLDG 3000 AEROMEDICAL
THANK YOU FOR INVITING ME TO WATCH, COL. BRUNSKY.
CERTAINLY, GENERAL.
"SUBJECT 65 THERE IS ONE OF OUR BEST. HE'S TAKEN TO THE TRAINING FAIRLY QUICKLY."
"HE'S ONE OF SIX THAT WILL BE GOING TO CANAVERAL THIS DECEMBER."

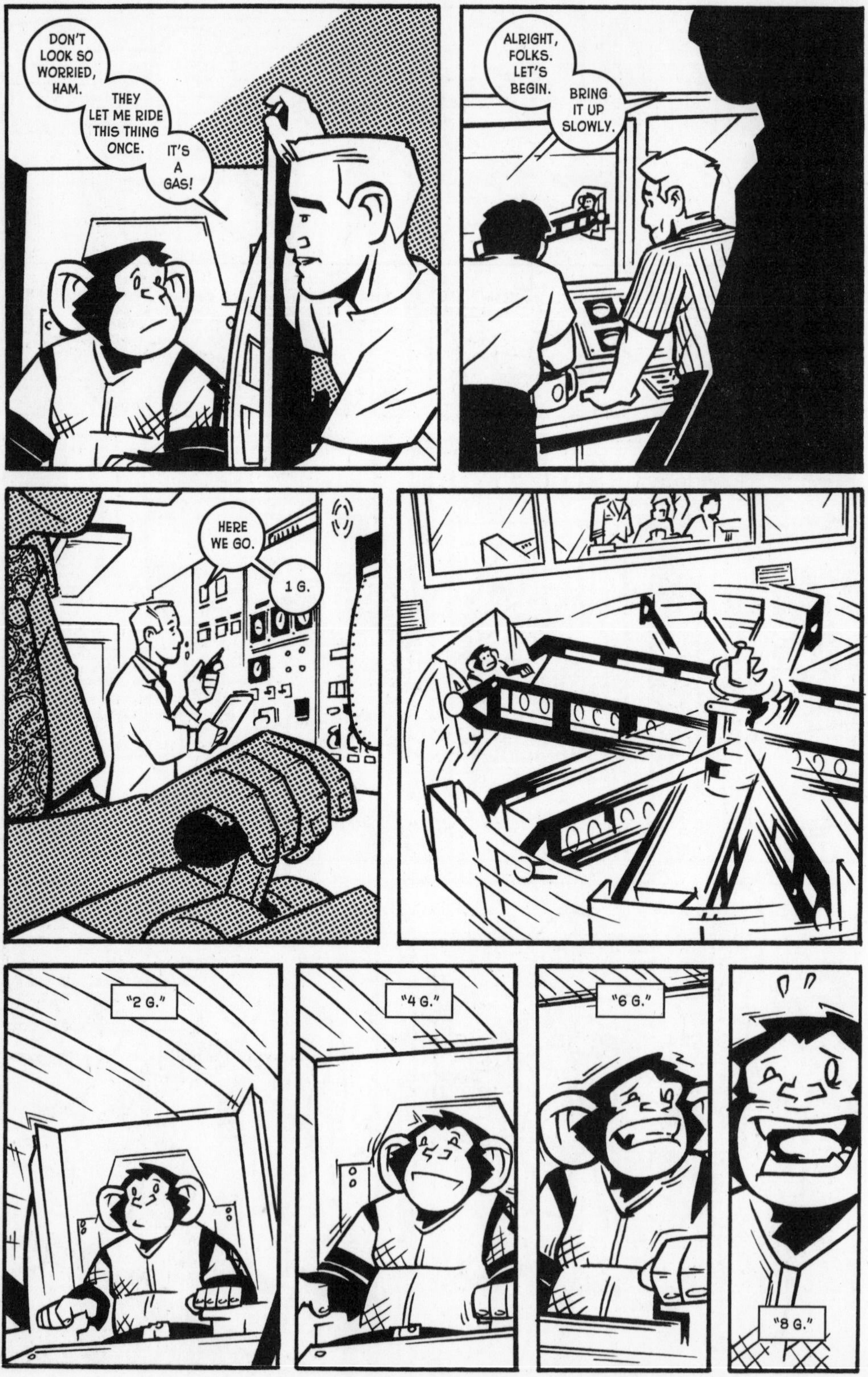
DON'T LOOK SO WORRIED, HAM.
THEY LET ME RIDE THIS THING ONCE.
IT'S A GAS!
ALRIGHT, FOLKS. LET'S BEGIN.
BRING IT UP SLOWLY.
HERE WE GO.
1 G.
"2 G."
"4 G."
"6 G."
"8 G."

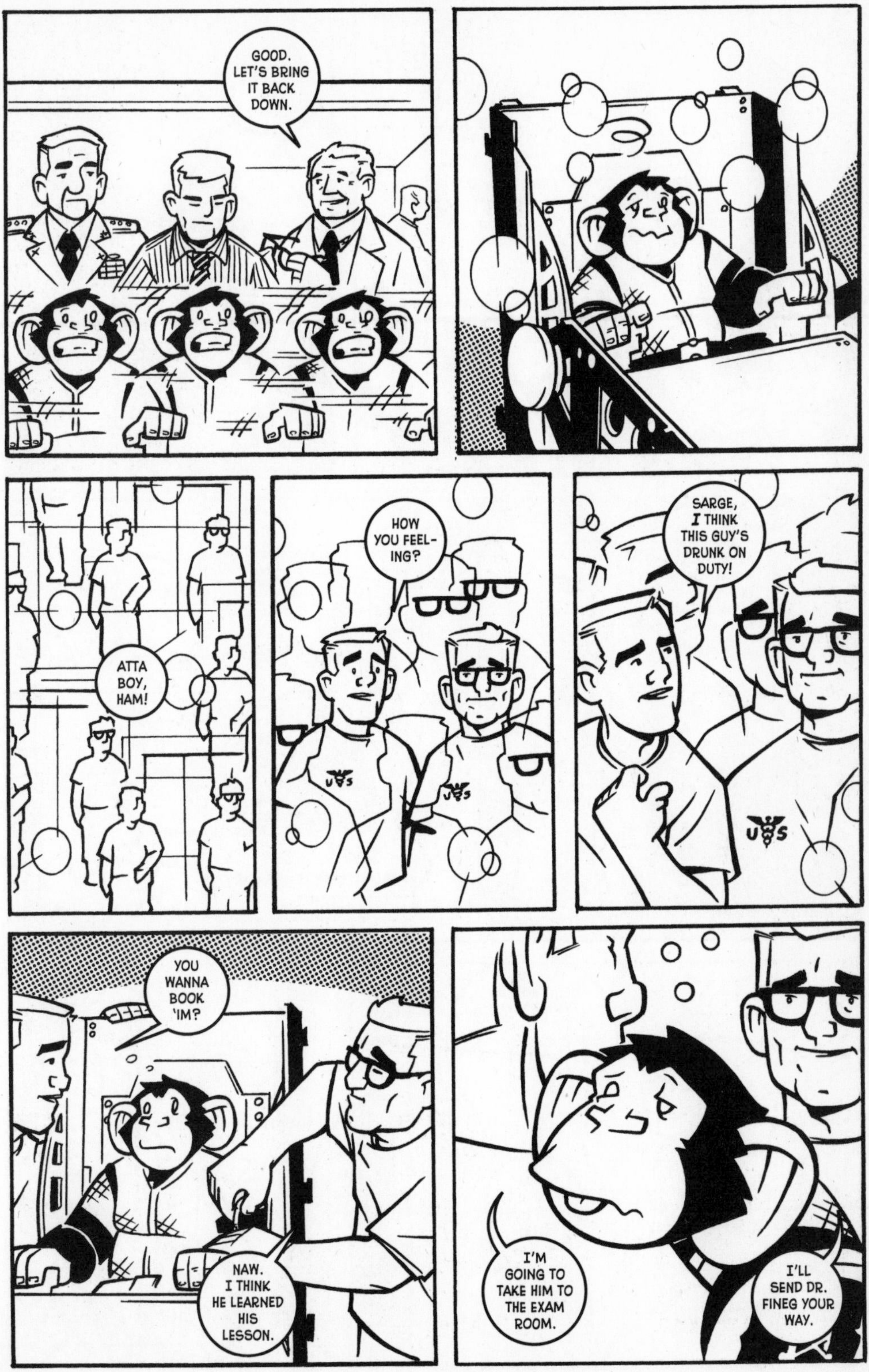
GOOD. LET'S BRING IT BACK DOWN.
ATTA BOY, HAM!
HOW YOU FEEL-ING?
SARGE, I THINK THIS GUY'S DRUNK ON DUTY!
YOU WANNA BOOK 'IM?
NAW. I THINK HE LEARNED HIS LESSON.
I'M GOING TO TAKE HIM TO THE EXAM ROOM.
I'LL SEND DR. FINEG YOUR WAY.

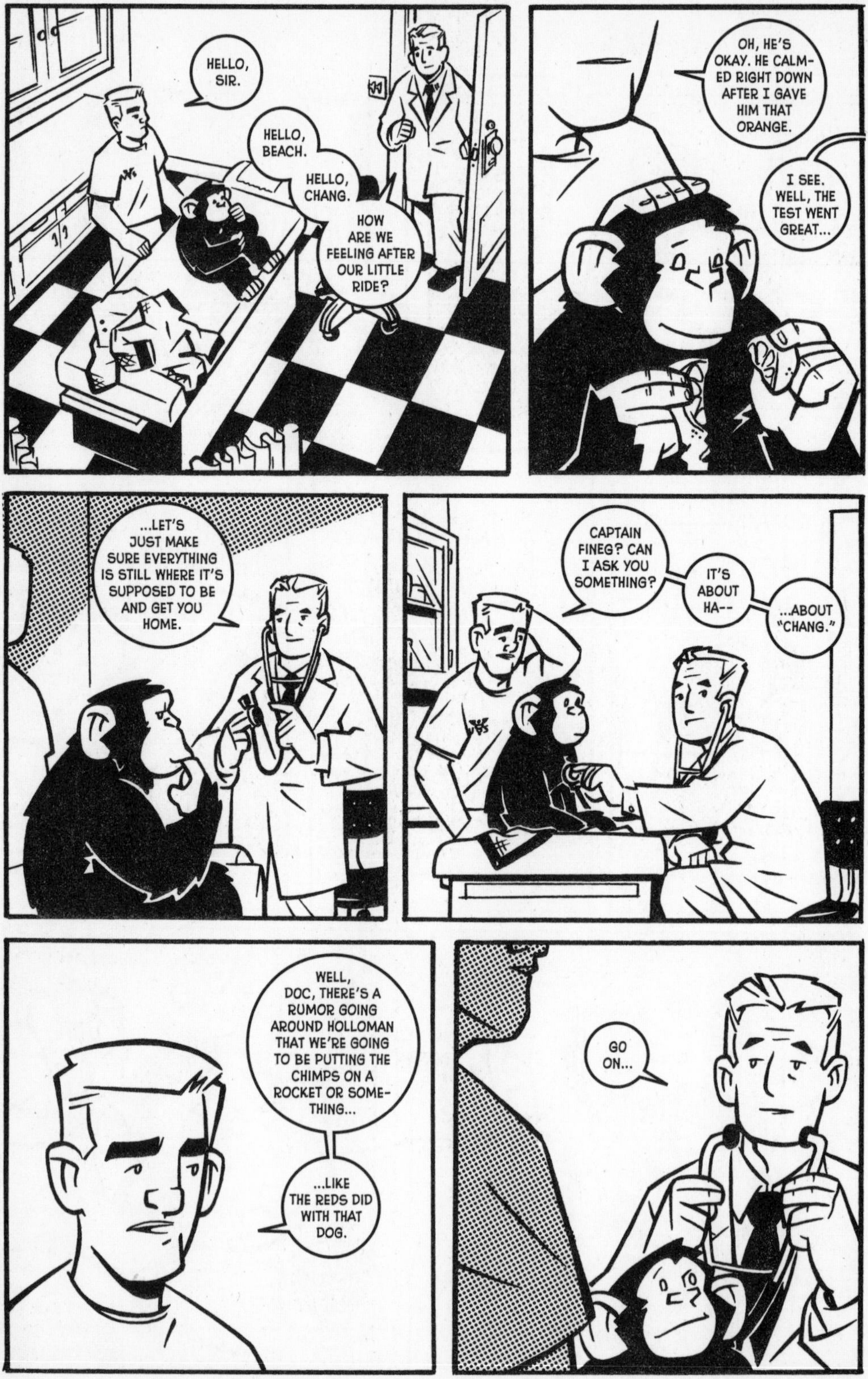
HELLO, SIR.
HELLO, BEACH.
HELLO, CHANG.
HOW ARE WE FEELING AFTER OUR LITTLE RIDE?
OH, HE'S OKAY. HE CALMED RIGHT DOWN AFTER I GAVE HIM THAT ORANGE.
I SEE. WELL, THE TEST WENT GREAT...
...LET'S JUST MAKE SURE EVERYTHING IS STILL WHERE IT'S SUPPOSED TO BE AND GET YOU HOME.
CAPTAIN FINEG? CAN I ASK YOU SOMETHING?
IT'S ABOUT HA--
...ABOUT "CHANG."
WELL, DOC, THERE'S A RUMOR GOING AROUND HOLLOMAN THAT WE'RE GOING TO BE PUTTING THE CHIMPS ON A ROCKET OR SOMETHING...
...LIKE THE REDS DID WITH THAT DOG.
GO ON...

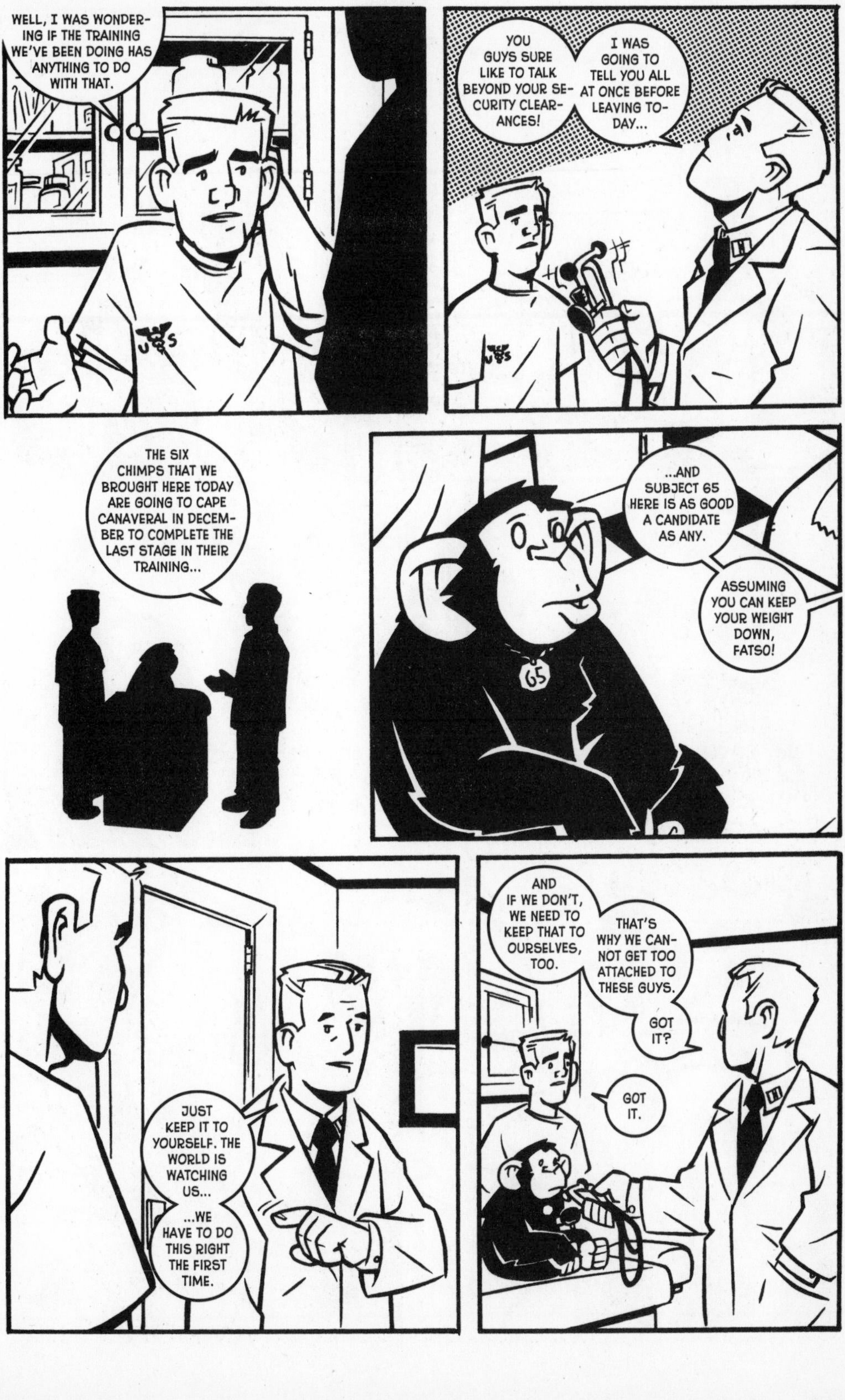
WELL, I WAS WONDERING IF THE TRAINING WE'VE BEEN DOING HAS ANYTHING TO DO WITH THAT.
YOU GUYS SURE LIKE TO TALK BEYOND YOUR SECURITY CLEARANCES!
I WAS GOING TO TELL YOU ALL AT ONCE BEFORE LEAVING TODAY...
THE SIX CHIMPS THAT WE BROUGHT HERE TODAY ARE GOING TO CAPE CANAVERAL IN DECEMBER TO COMPLETE THE LAST STAGE IN THEIR TRAINING...
...AND SUBJECT 65 HERE IS AS GOOD A CANDIDATE AS ANY.
65
ASSUMING YOU CAN KEEP YOUR WEIGHT DOWN, FATSO!
JUST KEEP IT TO YOURSELF. THE WORLD IS WATCHING US...
...WE HAVE TO DO THIS RIGHT THE FIRST TIME.
AND IF WE DON'T, WE NEED TO KEEP THAT TO OURSELVES, TOO.
THAT'S WHY WE CANNOT GET TOO ATTACHED TO THESE GUYS.
GOT IT?
GOT IT.

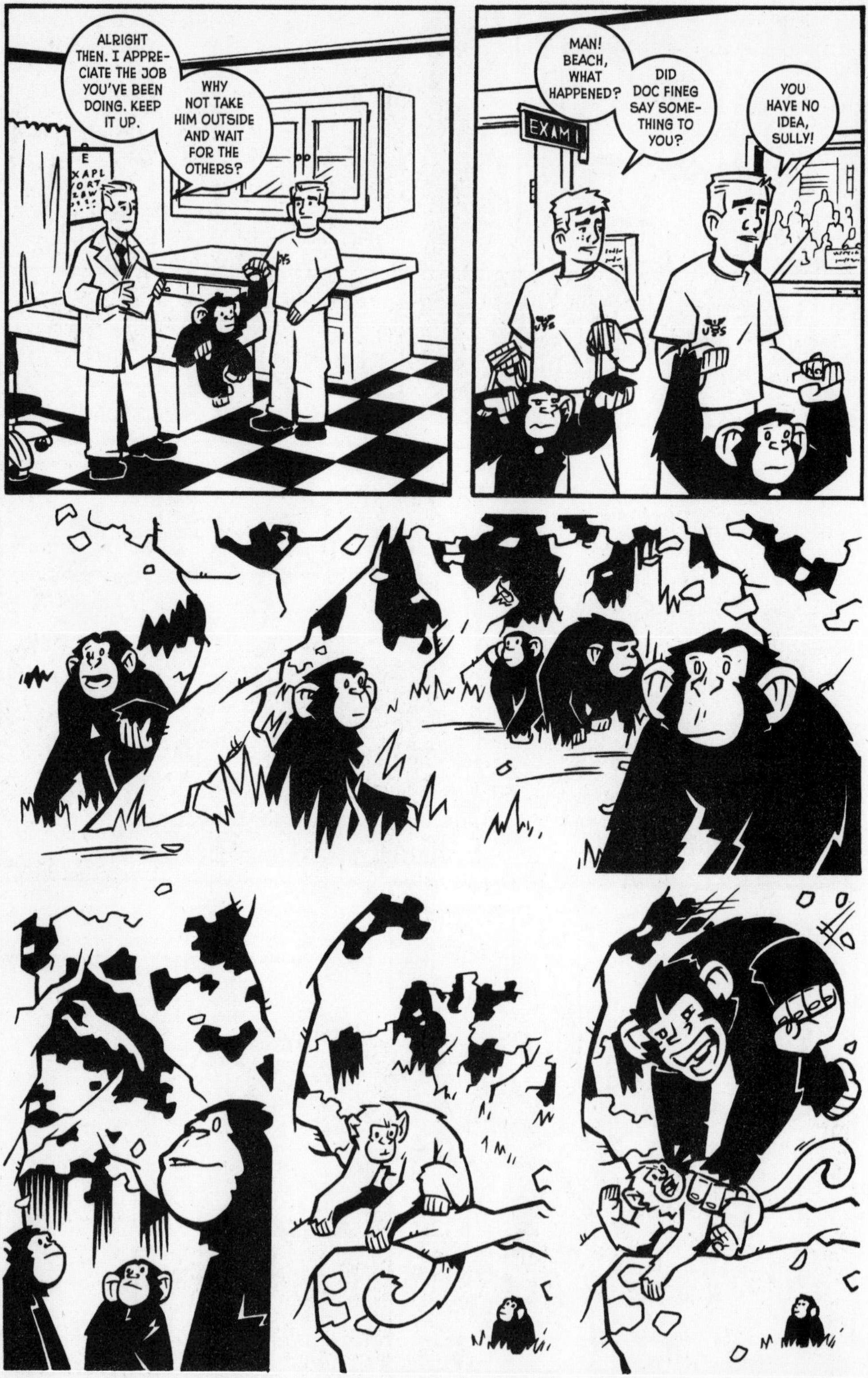
ALRIGHT THEN. I APPRECIATE THE JOB YOU'VE BEEN DOING. KEEP IT UP.
WHY NOT TAKE HIM OUTSIDE AND WAIT FOR THE OTHERS?
EXAM 1
MAN! BEACH, WHAT HAPPENED?
DID DOC FINEG SAY SOMETHING TO YOU?
YOU HAVE NO IDEA, SULLY!

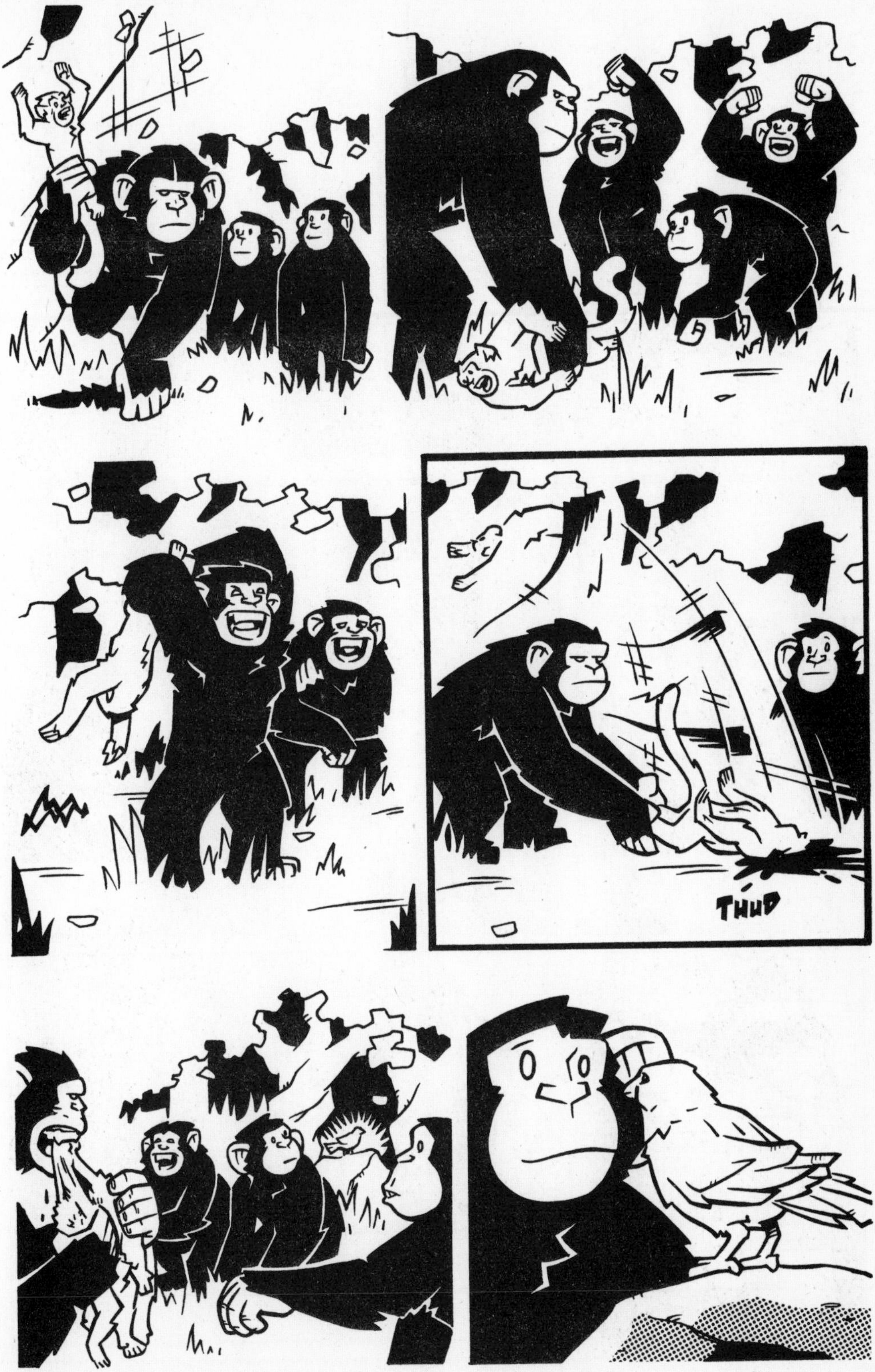
THUD

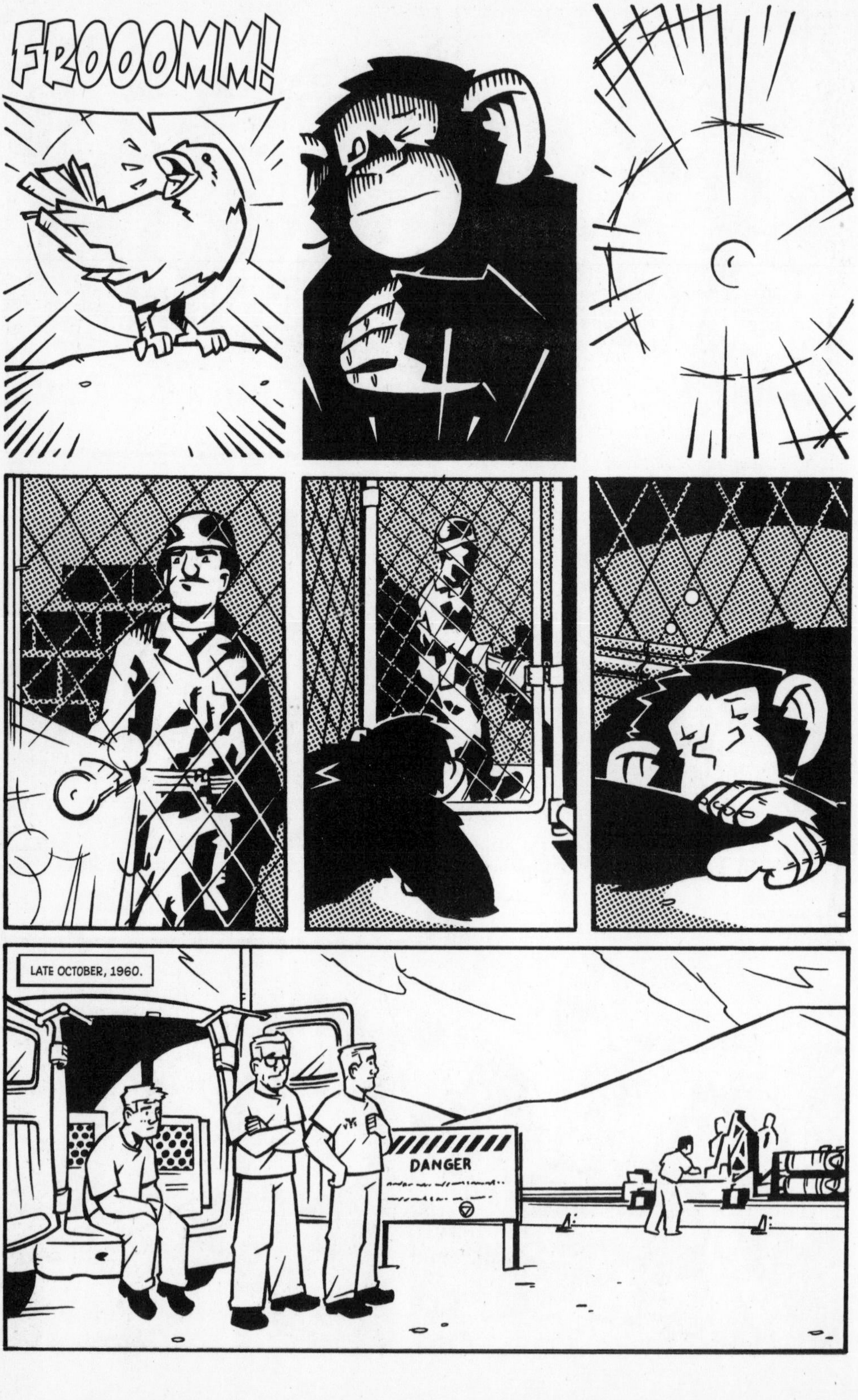
FROOOMM!
LATE OCTOBER, 1960.
DANGER

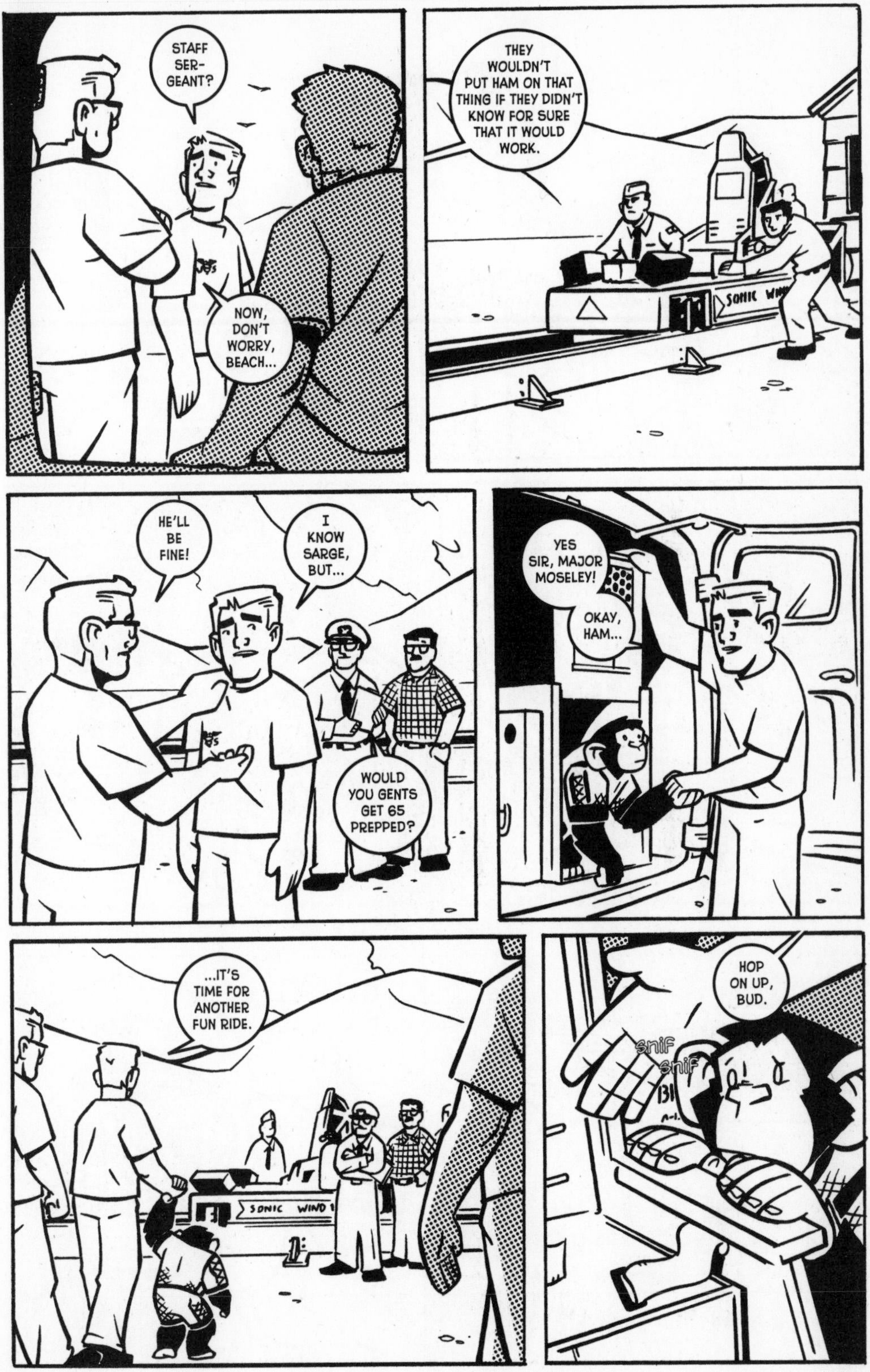
STAFF SER-GEANT?
NOW, DON'T WORRY, BEACH...
THEY WOULDN'T PUT HAM ON THAT THING IF THEY DIDN'T KNOW FOR SURE THAT IT WOULD WORK.
SONIC WIND
HE'LL BE FINE!
I KNOW SARGE, BUT...
WOULD YOU GENTS GET 65 PREPPED?
YES SIR, MAJOR MOSELEY!
OKAY, HAM...
...IT'S TIME FOR ANOTHER FUN RIDE.
SONIC WIND
HOP ON UP, BUD.
snif
snif

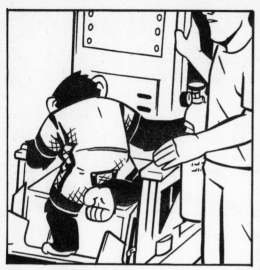

THAT'S A GOOD BOY.

DON'T WORRY, HAM. EVERY-THING'S JAKE.

I'LL BE WAITING AT THE OTHER END OF THE TRACK!

ALL PERSONNEL DOWNRAGE!

SONIC WIND 1

ACCEL-ERATION TEST IN 30.

T-MINUS 4...3...2...1...

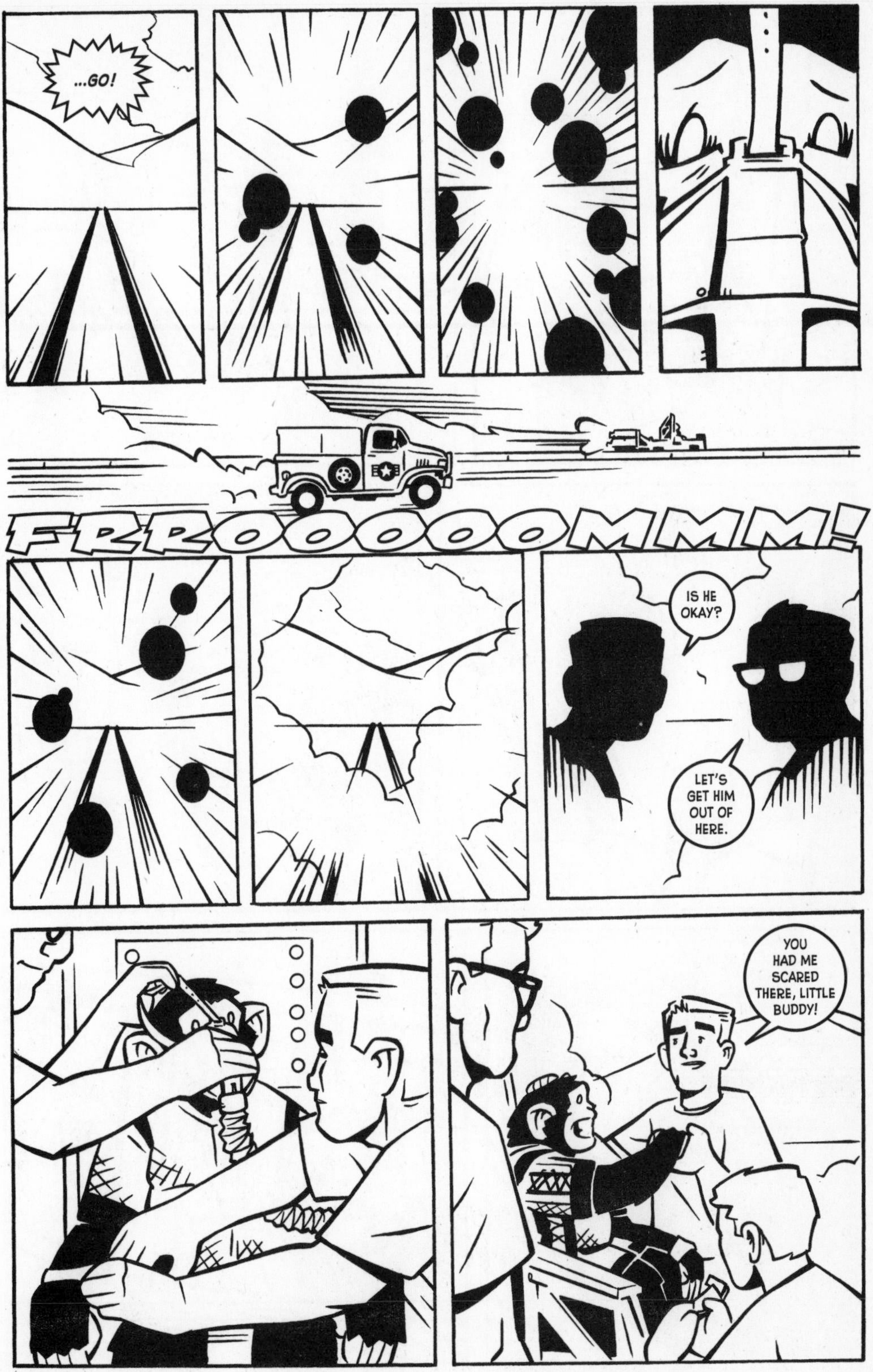
...GO!
FRROOOOOOMMMM!
IS HE OKAY?
LET'S GET HIM OUT OF HERE.
YOU HAD ME SCARED THERE, LITTLE BUDDY!

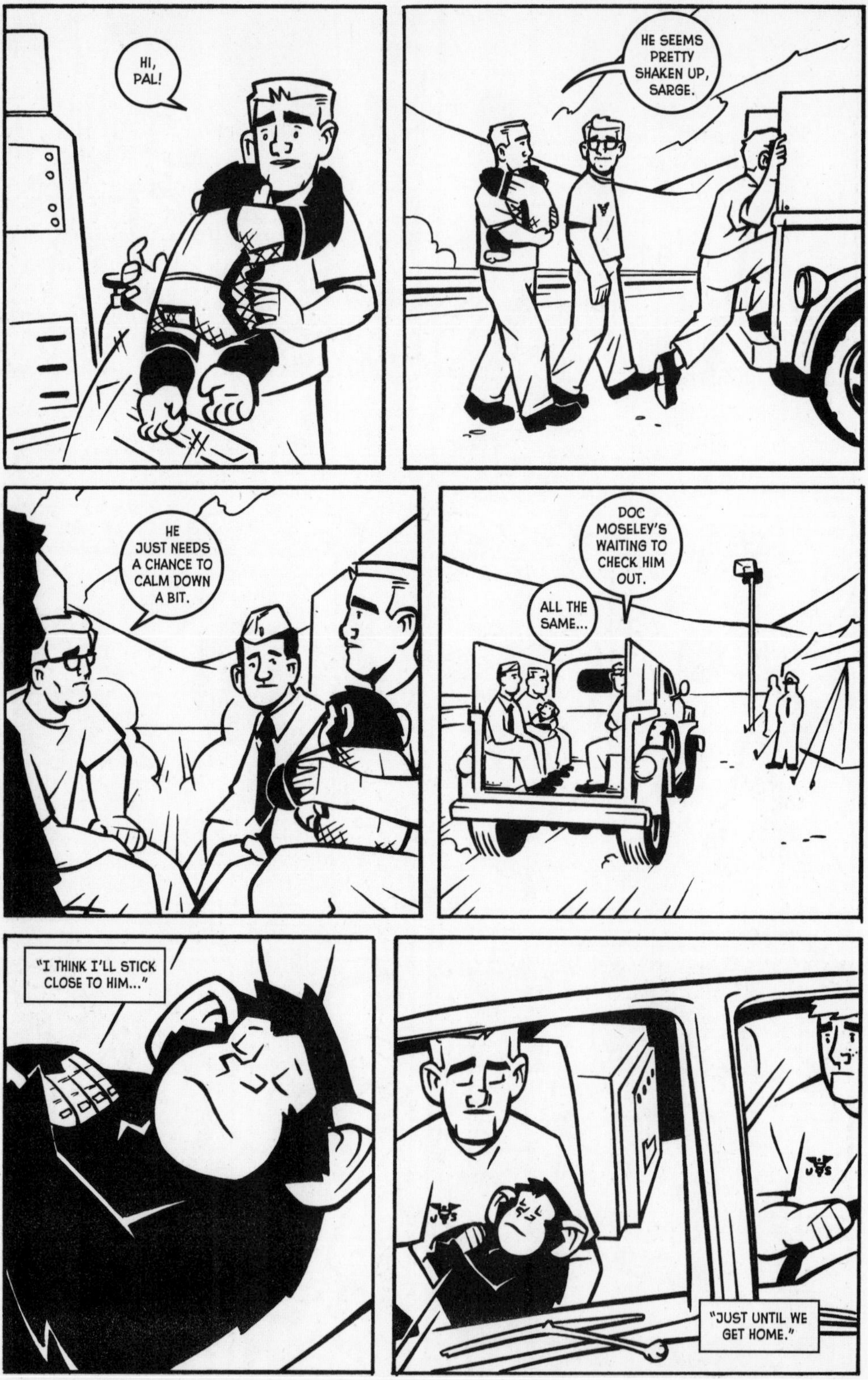
HI, PAL!
HE SEEMS PRETTY SHAKEN UP, SARGE.
HE JUST NEEDS A CHANCE TO CALM DOWN A BIT.
DOC MOSELEY'S WAITING TO CHECK HIM OUT.
ALL THE SAME...
"I THINK I'LL STICK CLOSE TO HIM..."
"JUST UNTIL WE GET HOME."

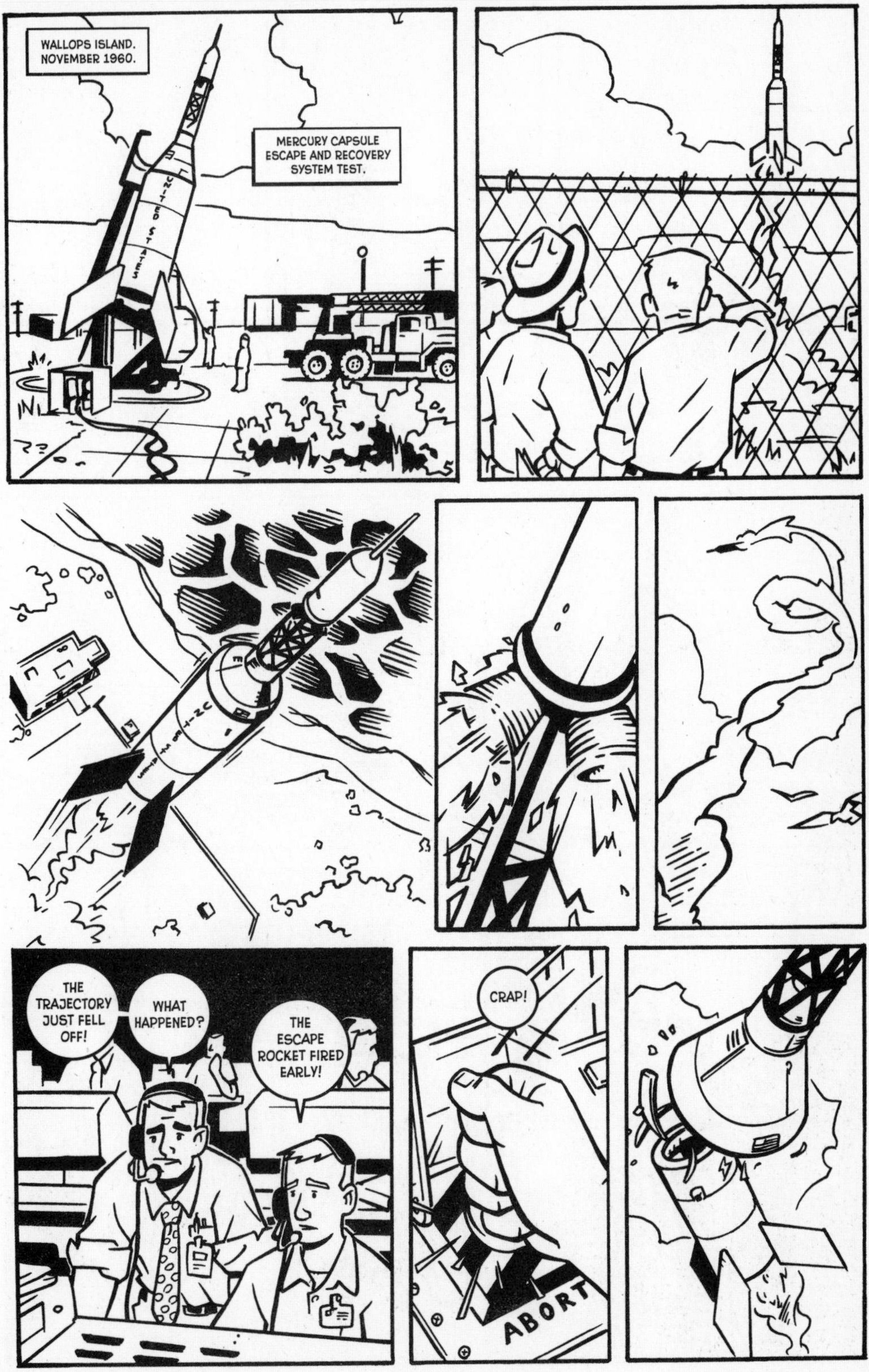
WALLOPS ISLAND. NOVEMBER 1960.
MERCURY CAPSULE ESCAPE AND RECOVERY SYSTEM TEST.
UNITED STATES
THE TRAJECTORY JUST FELL OFF!
WHAT HAPPENED?
THE ESCAPE ROCKET FIRED EARLY!
CRAP!
ABORT

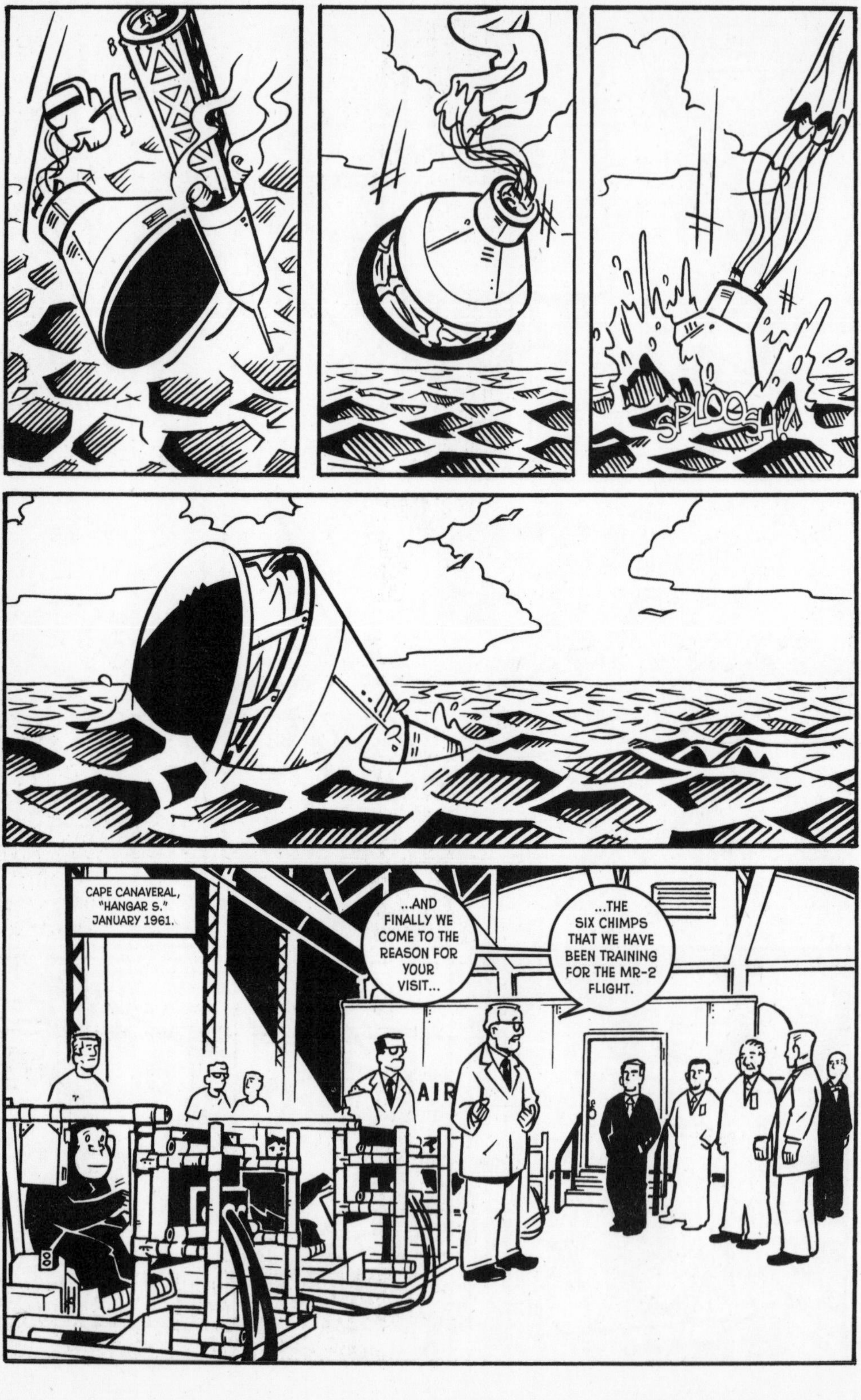
SPLOOSH!
CAPE CANAVERAL, "HANGAR S." JANUARY 1961.
...AND FINALLY WE COME TO THE REASON FOR YOUR VISIT...
...THE SIX CHIMPS THAT WE HAVE BEEN TRAINING FOR THE MR-2 FLIGHT.
AIR

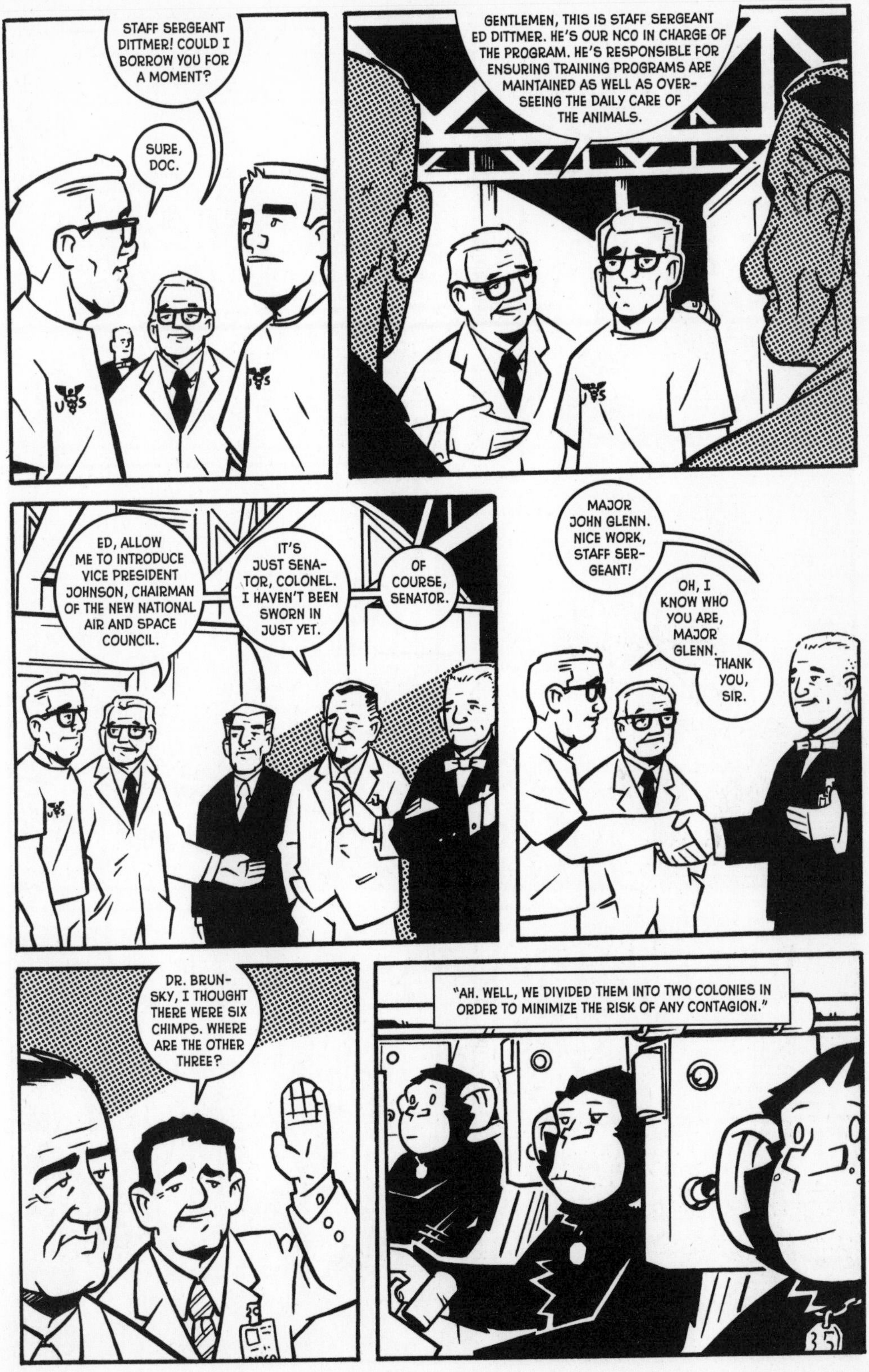
STAFF SERGEANT DITTMER! COULD I BORROW YOU FOR A MOMENT?
SURE, DOC.
GENTLEMEN, THIS IS STAFF SERGEANT ED DITTMER. HE'S OUR NCO IN CHARGE OF THE PROGRAM. HE'S RESPONSIBLE FOR ENSURING TRAINING PROGRAMS ARE MAINTAINED AS WELL AS OVER-SEEING THE DAILY CARE OF THE ANIMALS.
ED, ALLOW ME TO INTRODUCE VICE PRESIDENT JOHNSON, CHAIRMAN OF THE NEW NATIONAL AIR AND SPACE COUNCIL.
IT'S JUST SENA-TOR, COLONEL. I HAVEN'T BEEN SWORN IN JUST YET.
OF COURSE, SENATOR.
MAJOR JOHN GLENN. NICE WORK, STAFF SER-GEANT!
OH, I KNOW WHO YOU ARE, MAJOR GLENN.
THANK YOU, SIR.
DR. BRUN-SKY, I THOUGHT THERE WERE SIX CHIMPS. WHERE ARE THE OTHER THREE?
"AH. WELL, WE DIVIDED THEM INTO TWO COLONIES IN ORDER TO MINIMIZE THE RISK OF ANY CONTAGION."

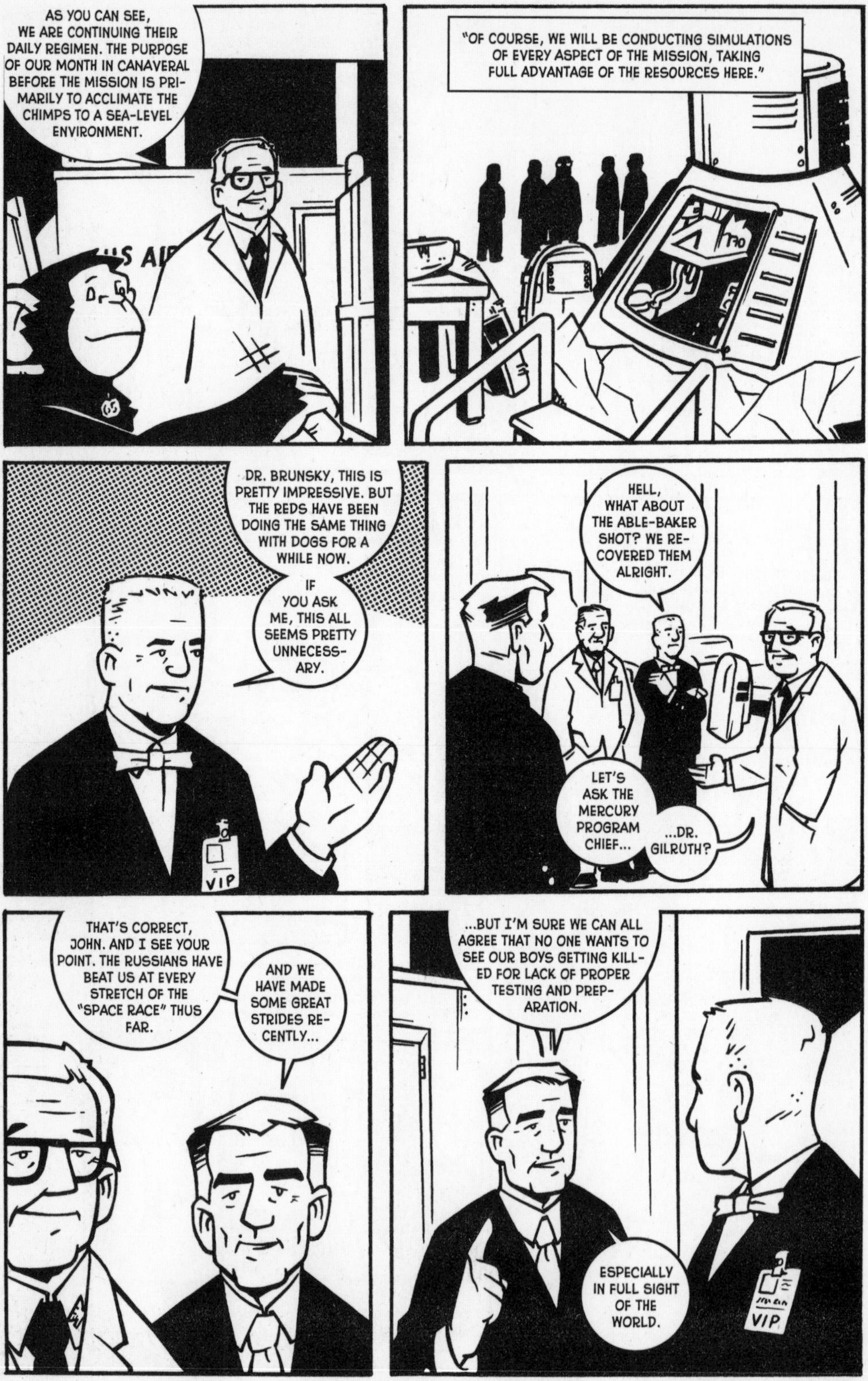
AS YOU CAN SEE, WE ARE CONTINUING THEIR DAILY REGIMEN. THE PURPOSE OF OUR MONTH IN CANAVERAL BEFORE THE MISSION IS PRIMARILY TO ACCLIMATE THE CHIMPS TO A SEA-LEVEL ENVIRONMENT.
"OF COURSE, WE WILL BE CONDUCTING SIMULATIONS OF EVERY ASPECT OF THE MISSION, TAKING FULL ADVANTAGE OF THE RESOURCES HERE."
DR. BRUNSKY, THIS IS PRETTY IMPRESSIVE. BUT THE REDS HAVE BEEN DOING THE SAME THING WITH DOGS FOR A WHILE NOW.
IF YOU ASK ME, THIS ALL SEEMS PRETTY UNNECESSARY.
VIP
HELL, WHAT ABOUT THE ABLE-BAKER SHOT? WE RECOVERED THEM ALRIGHT.
LET'S ASK THE MERCURY PROGRAM CHIEF...
...DR. GILRUTH?
THAT'S CORRECT, JOHN. AND I SEE YOUR POINT. THE RUSSIANS HAVE BEAT US AT EVERY STRETCH OF THE "SPACE RACE" THUS FAR.
AND WE HAVE MADE SOME GREAT STRIDES RECENTLY...
...BUT I'M SURE WE CAN ALL AGREE THAT NO ONE WANTS TO SEE OUR BOYS GETTING KILLED FOR LACK OF PROPER TESTING AND PREPARATION.
ESPECIALLY IN FULL SIGHT OF THE WORLD.
VIP

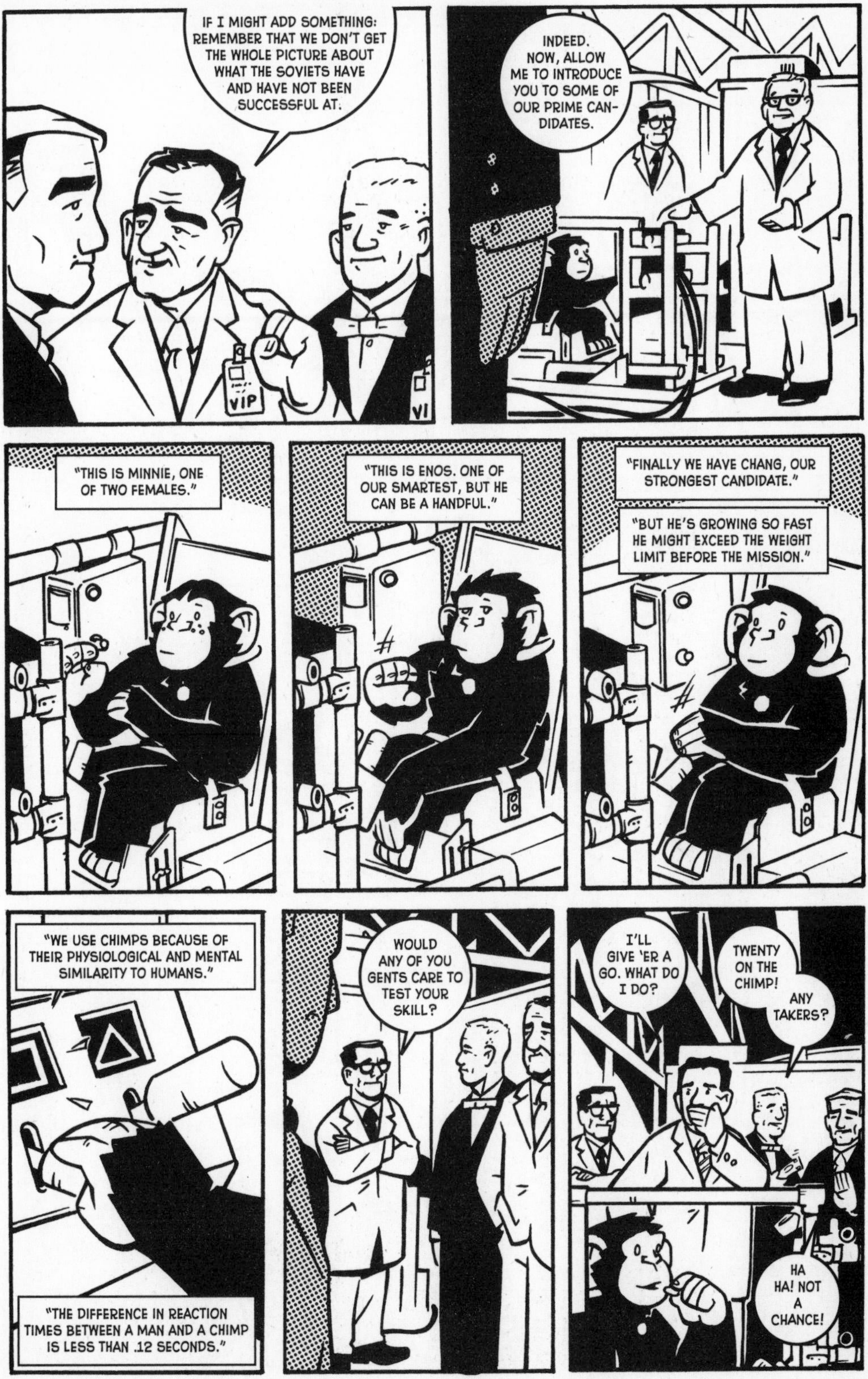
IF I MIGHT ADD SOMETHING: REMEMBER THAT WE DON'T GET THE WHOLE PICTURE ABOUT WHAT THE SOVIETS HAVE AND HAVE NOT BEEN SUCCESSFUL AT.
VIP
INDEED. NOW, ALLOW ME TO INTRODUCE YOU TO SOME OF OUR PRIME CAN-DIDATES.
"THIS IS MINNIE, ONE OF TWO FEMALES."
"THIS IS ENOS. ONE OF OUR SMARTEST, BUT HE CAN BE A HANDFUL."
"FINALLY WE HAVE CHANG, OUR STRONGEST CANDIDATE."
"BUT HE'S GROWING SO FAST HE MIGHT EXCEED THE WEIGHT LIMIT BEFORE THE MISSION."
"WE USE CHIMPS BECAUSE OF THEIR PHYSIOLOGICAL AND MENTAL SIMILARITY TO HUMANS."
"THE DIFFERENCE IN REACTION TIMES BETWEEN A MAN AND A CHIMP IS LESS THAN .12 SECONDS."
WOULD ANY OF YOU GENTS CARE TO TEST YOUR SKILL?
I'LL GIVE 'ER A GO. WHAT DO I DO?
TWENTY ON THE CHIMP!
ANY TAKERS?
HA HA! NOT A CHANCE!

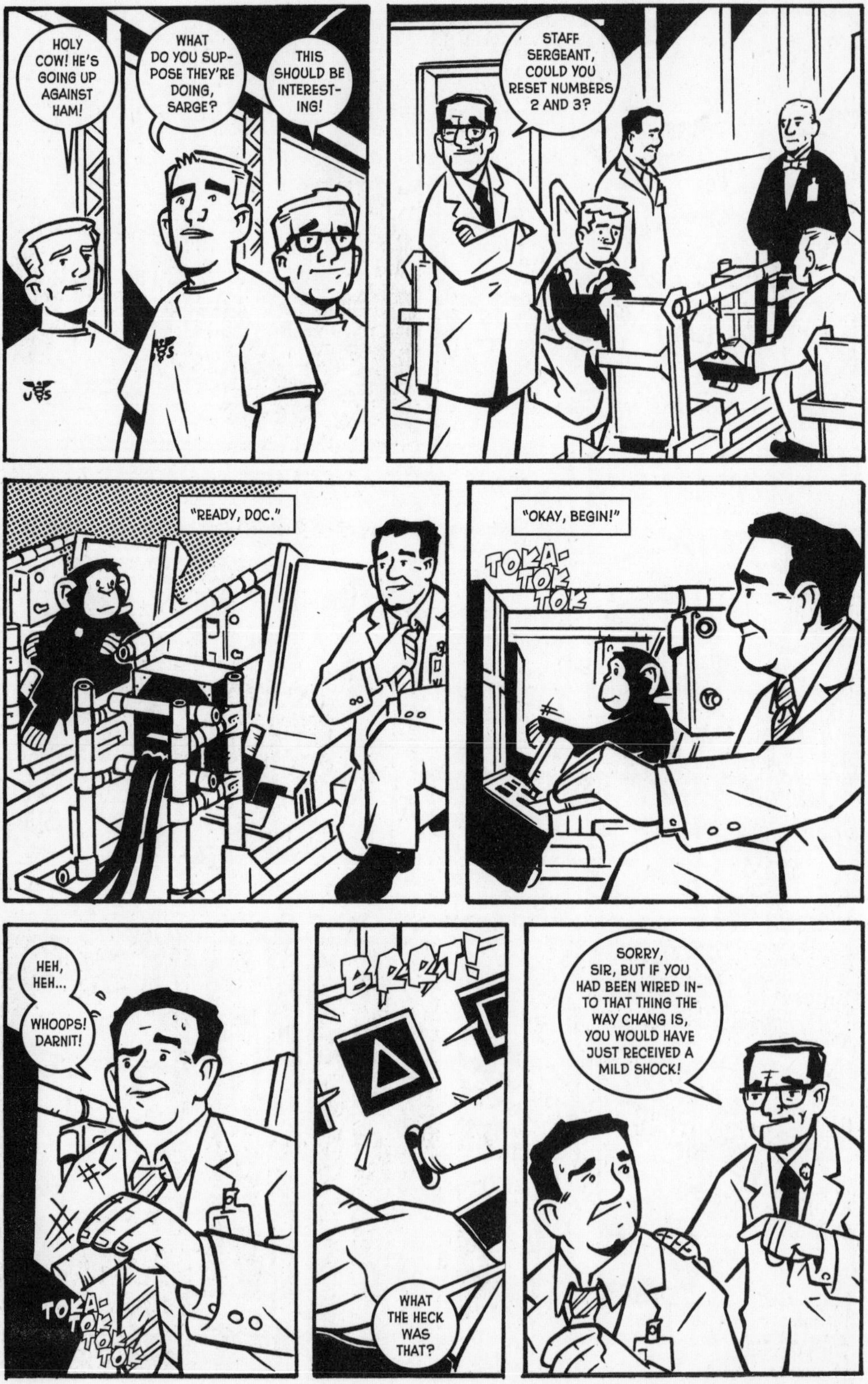
HOLY COW! HE'S GOING UP AGAINST HAM!
WHAT DO YOU SUPPOSE THEY'RE DOING, SARGE?
THIS SHOULD BE INTERESTING!
STAFF SERGEANT, COULD YOU RESET NUMBERS 2 AND 3?
"READY, DOC."
"OKAY, BEGIN!"
TOKA-TOK TOK
HEH, HEH...
WHOOPS! DARNIT!
TOKA-TOK TOK TOK
BRRT!
WHAT THE HECK WAS THAT?
SORRY, SIR, BUT IF YOU HAD BEEN WIRED INTO THAT THING THE WAY CHANG IS, YOU WOULD HAVE JUST RECEIVED A MILD SHOCK!

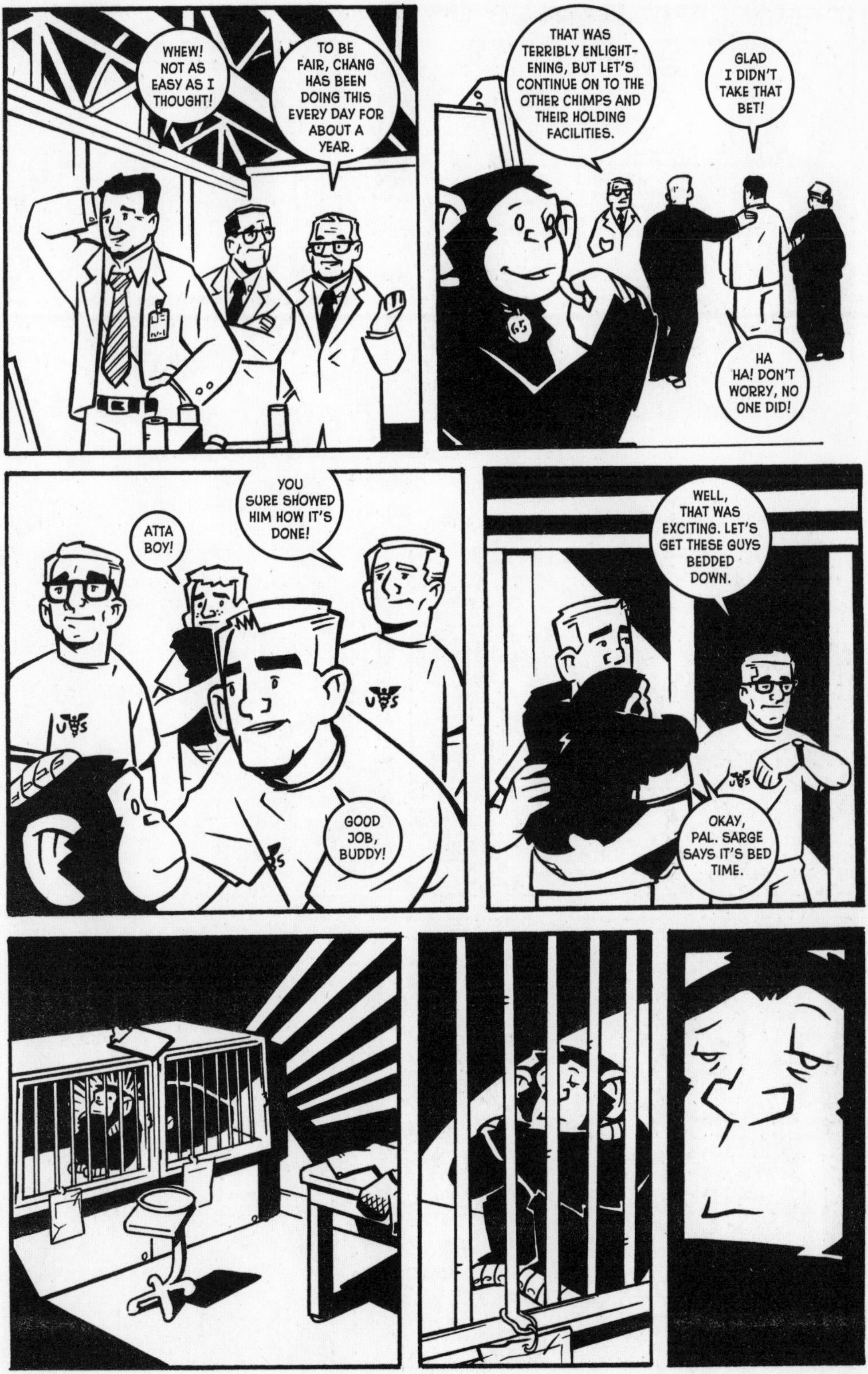
WHEW! NOT AS EASY AS I THOUGHT!
TO BE FAIR, CHANG HAS BEEN DOING THIS EVERY DAY FOR ABOUT A YEAR.
THAT WAS TERRIBLY ENLIGHT-ENING, BUT LET'S CONTINUE ON TO THE OTHER CHIMPS AND THEIR HOLDING FACILITIES.
GLAD I DIDN'T TAKE THAT BET!
HA HA! DON'T WORRY, NO ONE DID!
ATTA BOY!
YOU SURE SHOWED HIM HOW IT'S DONE!
GOOD JOB, BUDDY!
WELL, THAT WAS EXCITING. LET'S GET THESE GUYS BEDDED DOWN.
OKAY, PAL. SARGE SAYS IT'S BED TIME.

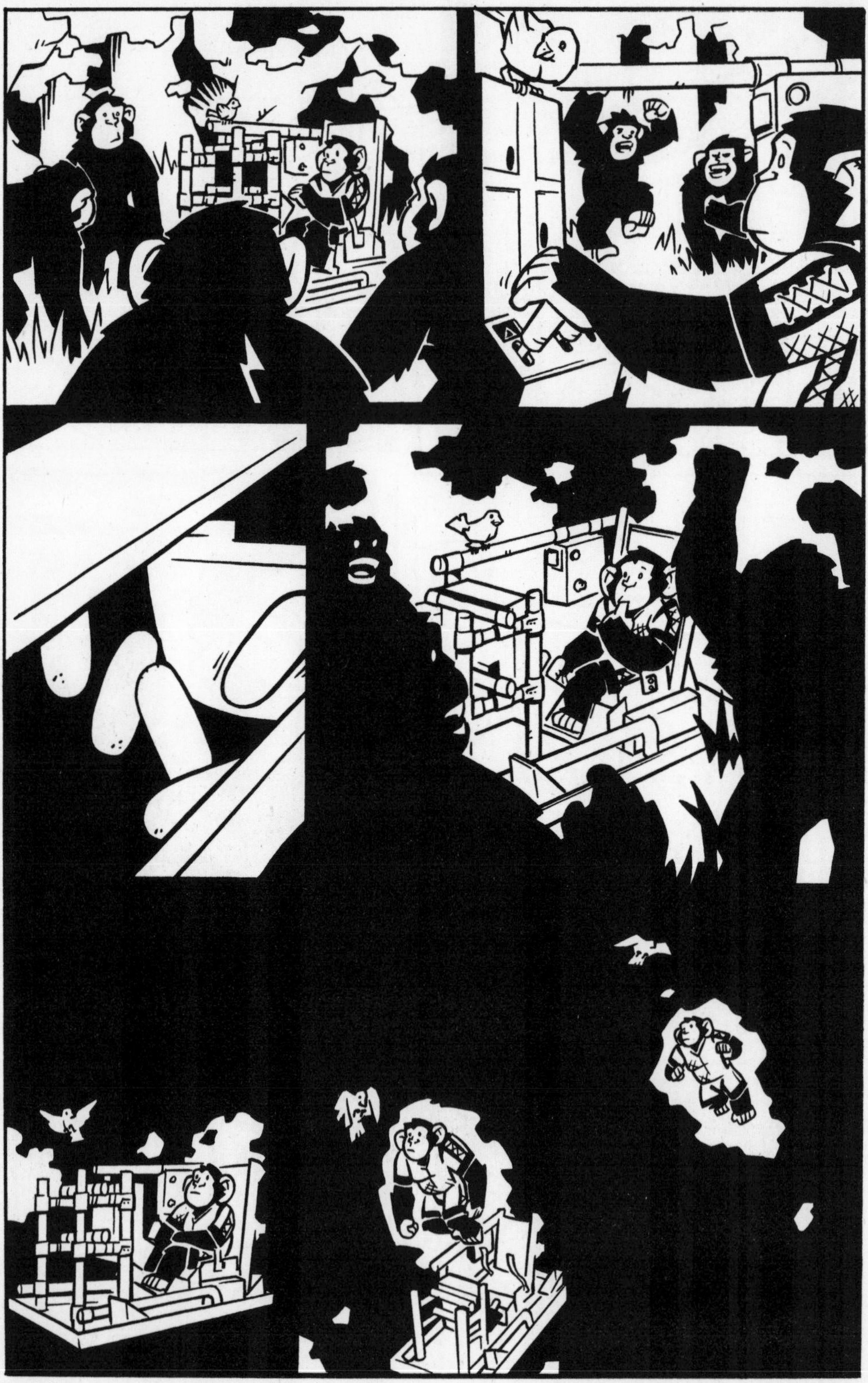

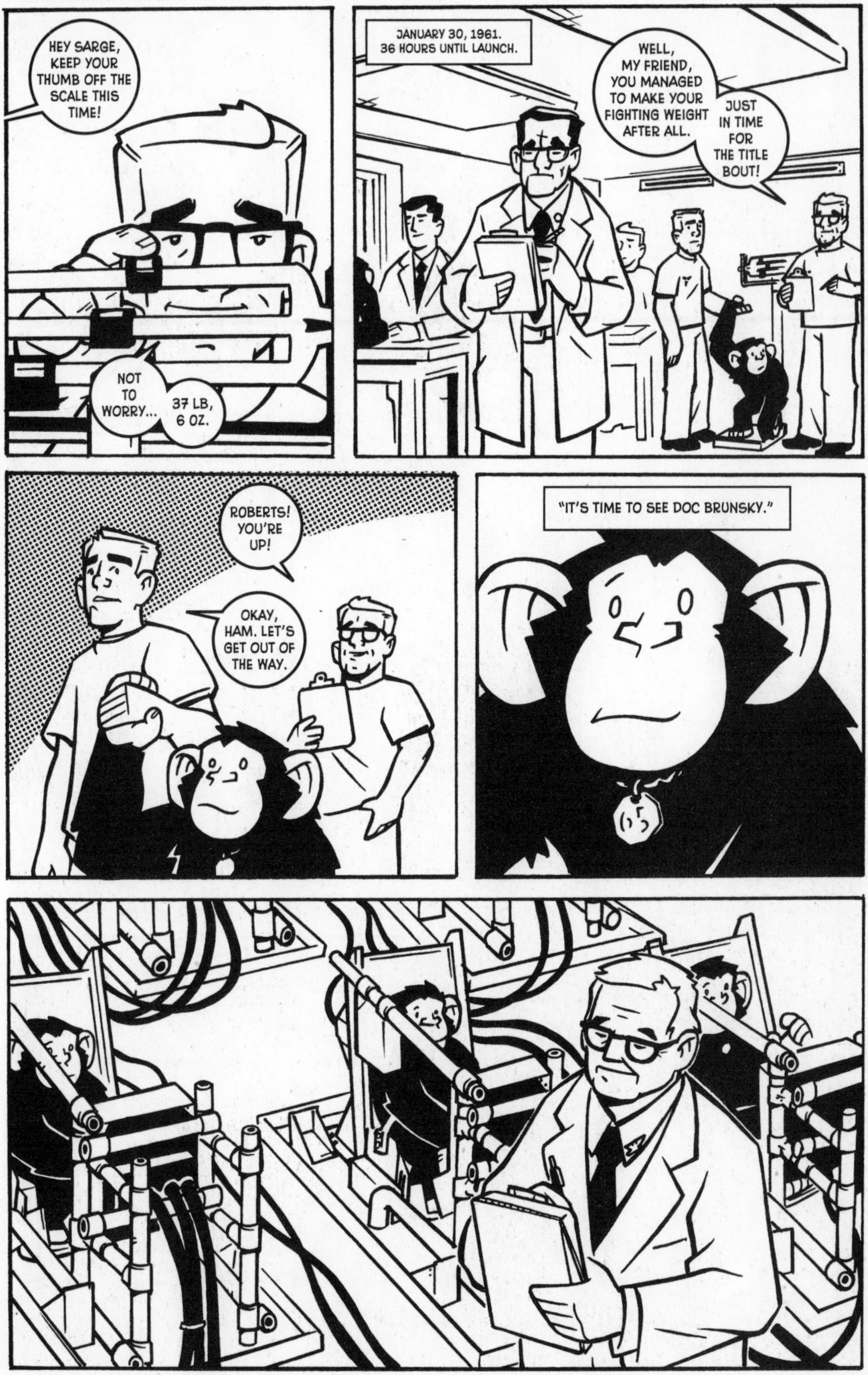
HEY SARGE, KEEP YOUR THUMB OFF THE SCALE THIS TIME!
NOT TO WORRY...
37 LB, 6 OZ.
JANUARY 30, 1961. 36 HOURS UNTIL LAUNCH.
WELL, MY FRIEND, YOU MANAGED TO MAKE YOUR FIGHTING WEIGHT AFTER ALL.
JUST IN TIME FOR THE TITLE BOUT!
ROBERTS! YOU'RE UP!
OKAY, HAM. LET'S GET OUT OF THE WAY.
"IT'S TIME TO SEE DOC BRUNSKY."

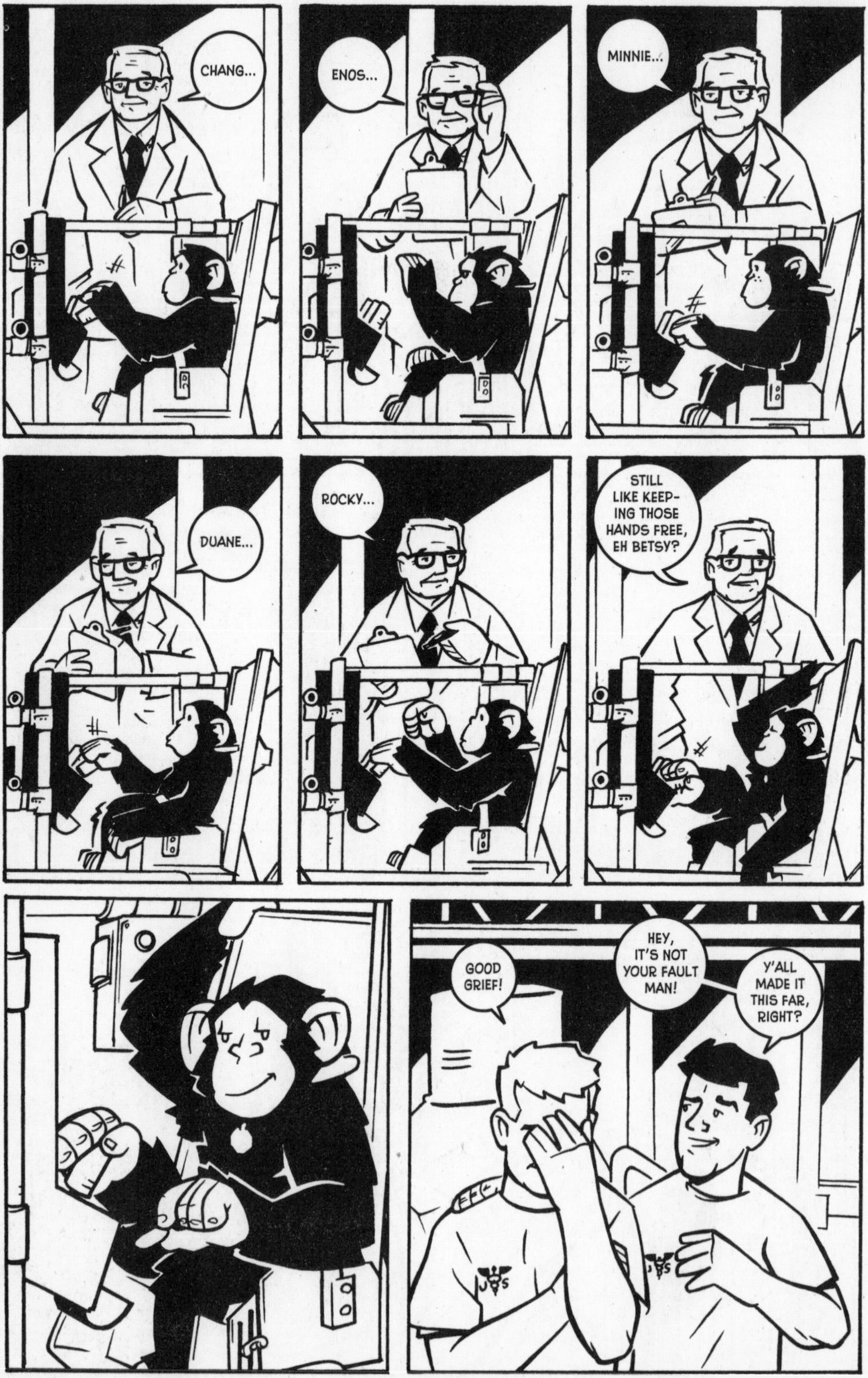
CHANG...
ENOS...
MINNIE...
DUANE...
ROCKY...
STILL LIKE KEEP-ING THOSE HANDS FREE, EH BETSY?
GOOD GRIEF!
HEY, IT'S NOT YOUR FAULT MAN!
Y'ALL MADE IT THIS FAR, RIGHT?

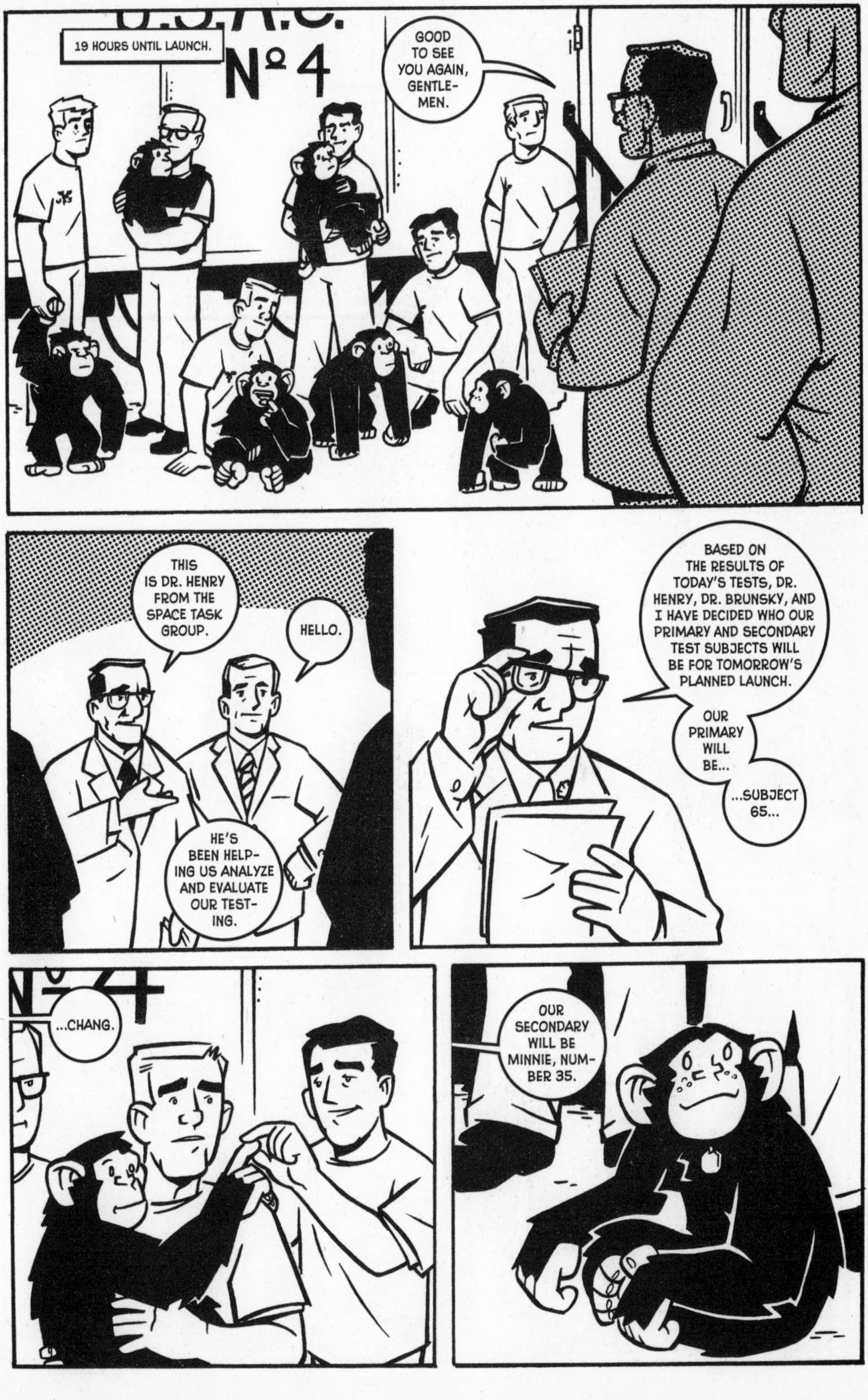
19 HOURS UNTIL LAUNCH.
Nº 4
GOOD TO SEE YOU AGAIN, GENTLEMEN.
THIS IS DR. HENRY FROM THE SPACE TASK GROUP.
HELLO.
HE'S BEEN HELPING US ANALYZE AND EVALUATE OUR TESTING.
BASED ON THE RESULTS OF TODAY'S TESTS, DR. HENRY, DR. BRUNSKY, AND I HAVE DECIDED WHO OUR PRIMARY AND SECONDARY TEST SUBJECTS WILL BE FOR TOMORROW'S PLANNED LAUNCH.
OUR PRIMARY WILL BE...
...SUBJECT 65...
...CHANG.
OUR SECONDARY WILL BE MINNIE, NUMBER 35.

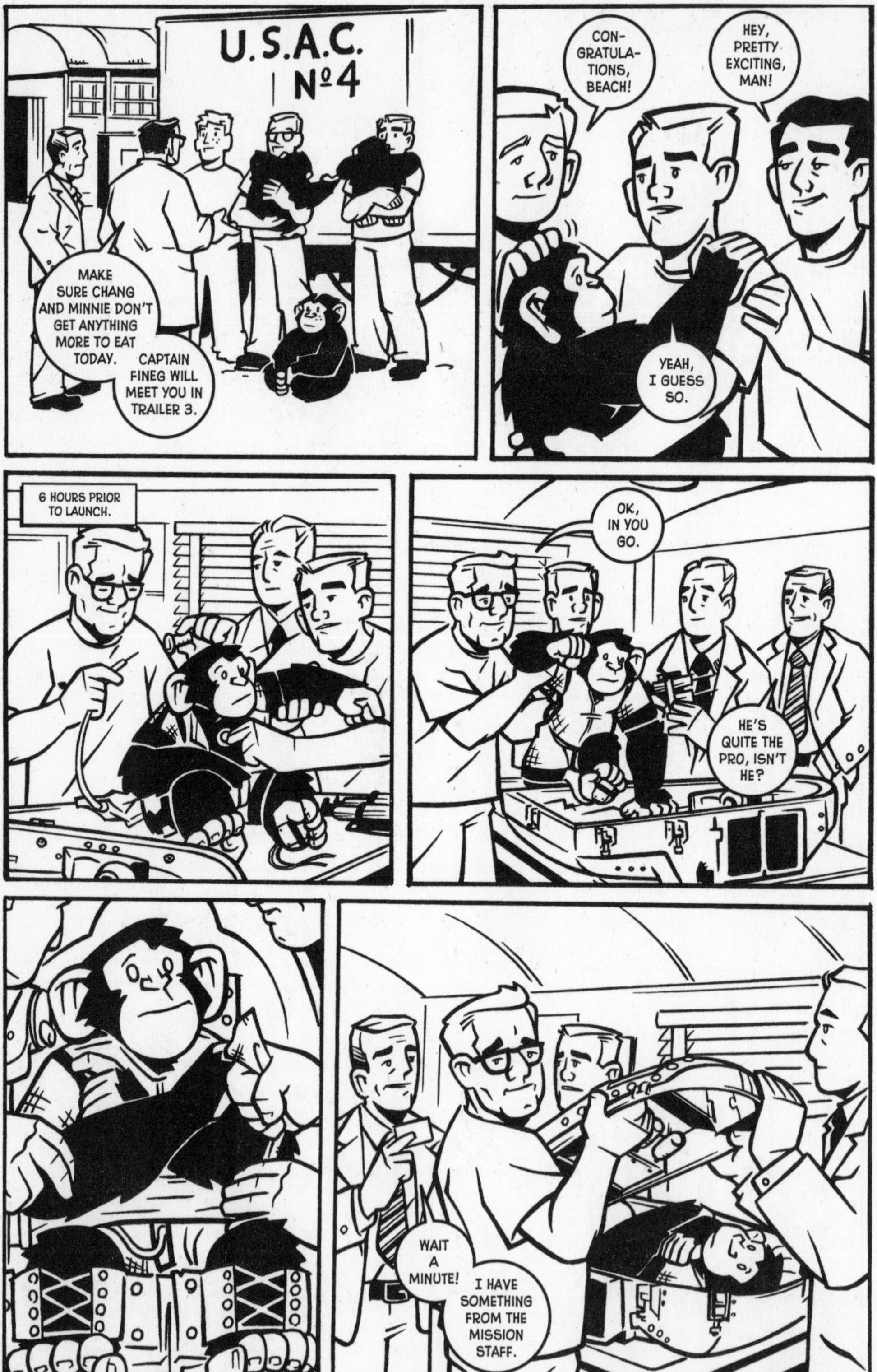
U.S.A.C. Nº4
MAKE SURE CHANG AND MINNIE DON'T GET ANYTHING MORE TO EAT TODAY.
CAPTAIN FINEG WILL MEET YOU IN TRAILER 3.
CON-GRATULA-TIONS, BEACH!
HEY, PRETTY EXCITING, MAN!
YEAH, I GUESS SO.
6 HOURS PRIOR TO LAUNCH.
OK, IN YOU GO.
HE'S QUITE THE PRO, ISN'T HE?
WAIT A MINUTE!
I HAVE SOMETHING FROM THE MISSION STAFF.

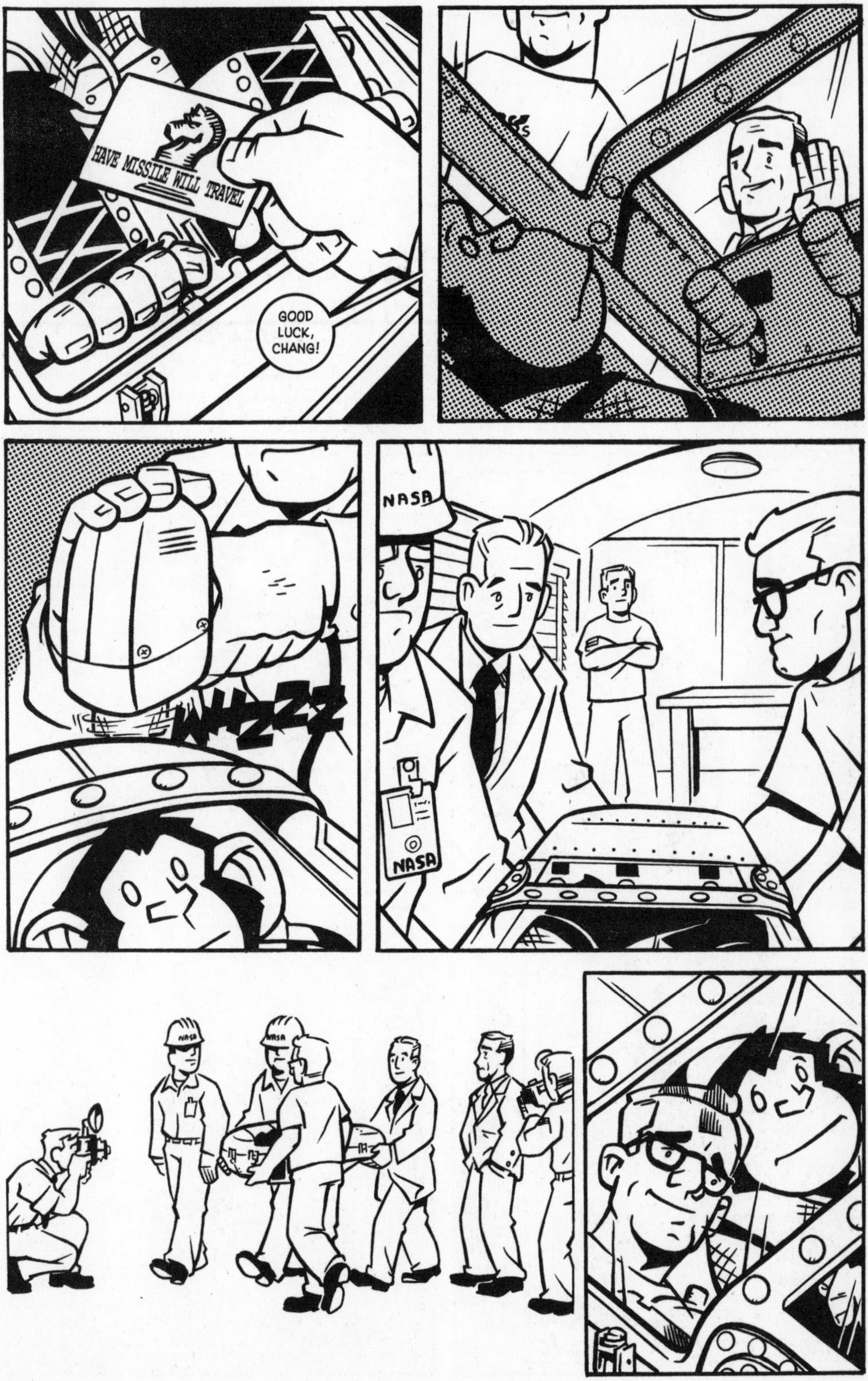
HAVE MISSILE WILL TRAVEL
GOOD LUCK, CHANG!
WHZZZ
NASA
NASA
NASA
NASA

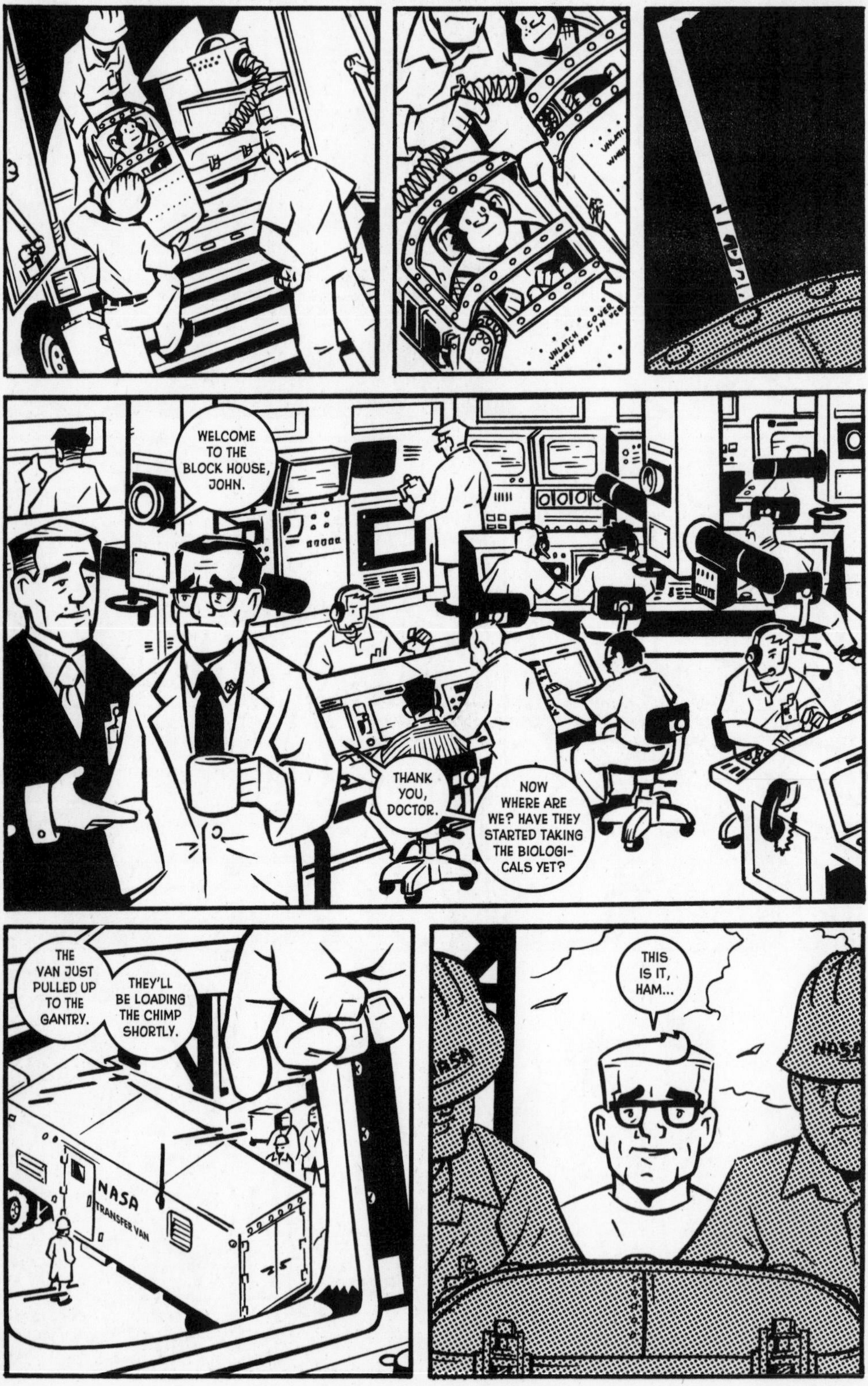
UNLATCH COVER WHEN NOT IN USE
WELCOME TO THE BLOCK HOUSE, JOHN.
THANK YOU, DOCTOR.
NOW WHERE ARE WE? HAVE THEY STARTED TAKING THE BIOLOGI-CALS YET?
THE VAN JUST PULLED UP TO THE GANTRY.
THEY'LL BE LOADING THE CHIMP SHORTLY.
NASA TRANSFER VAN
THIS IS IT, HAM...
NASA

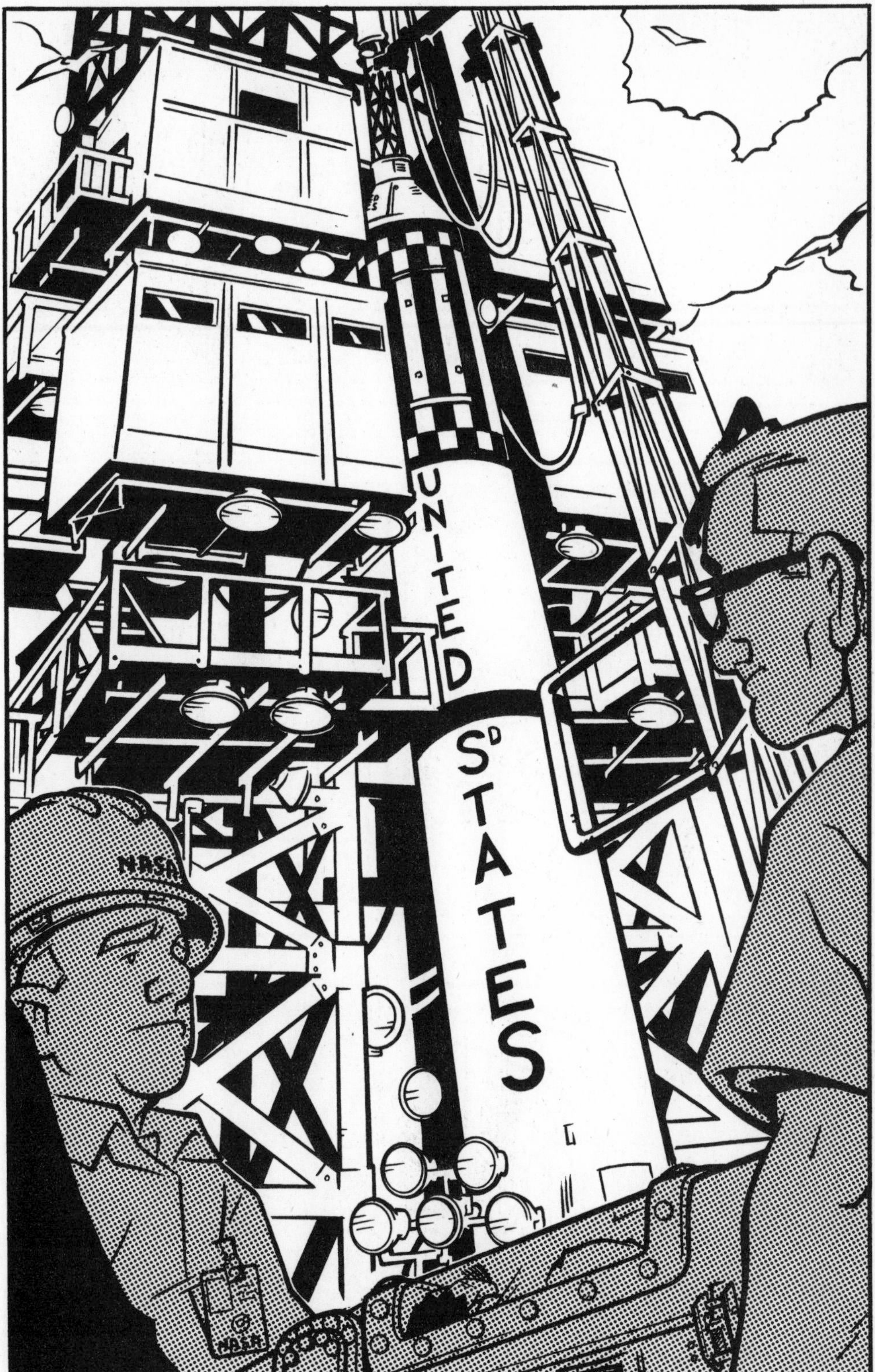
UNITED
STATES
NASA

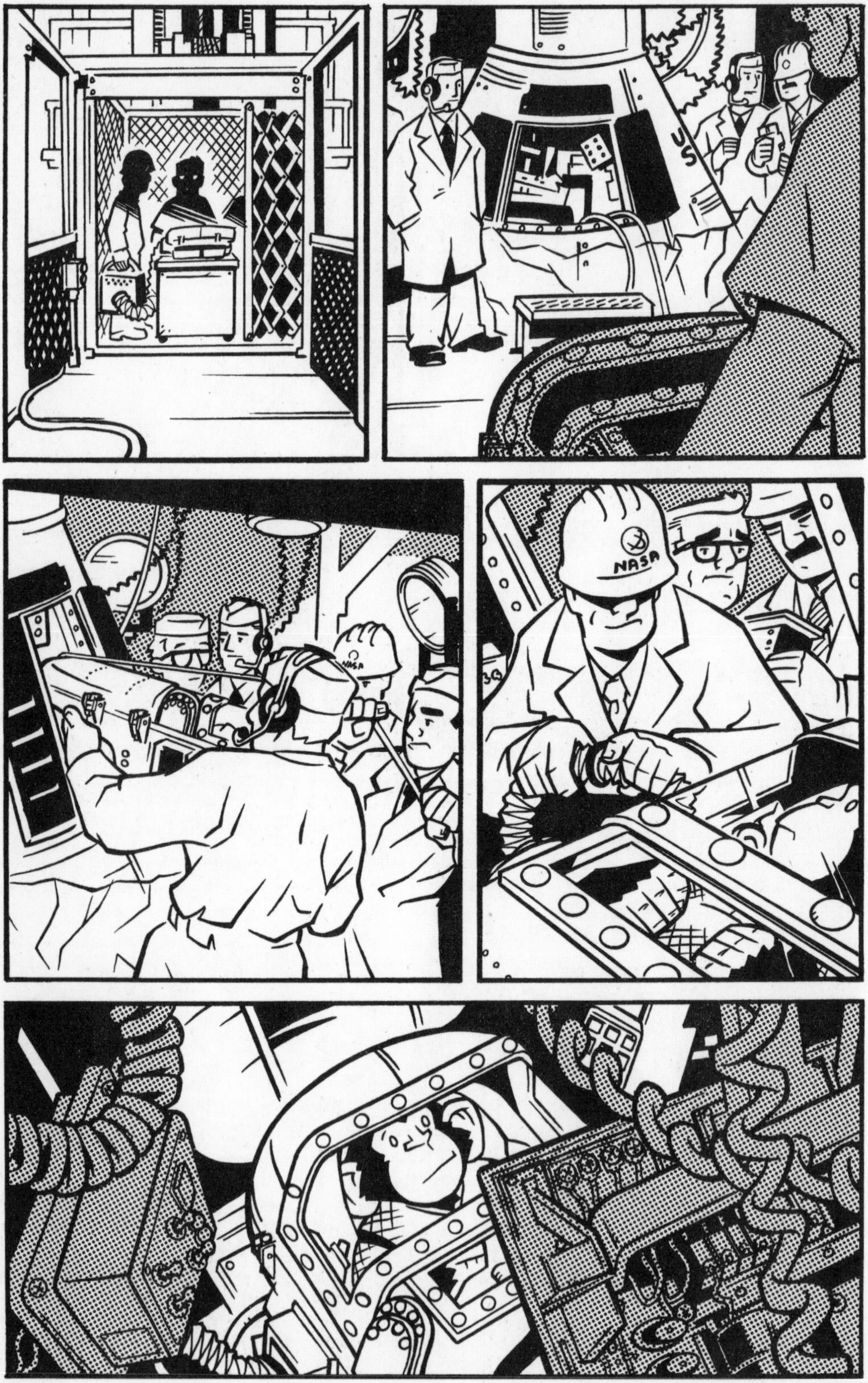
US
NASA
NASA

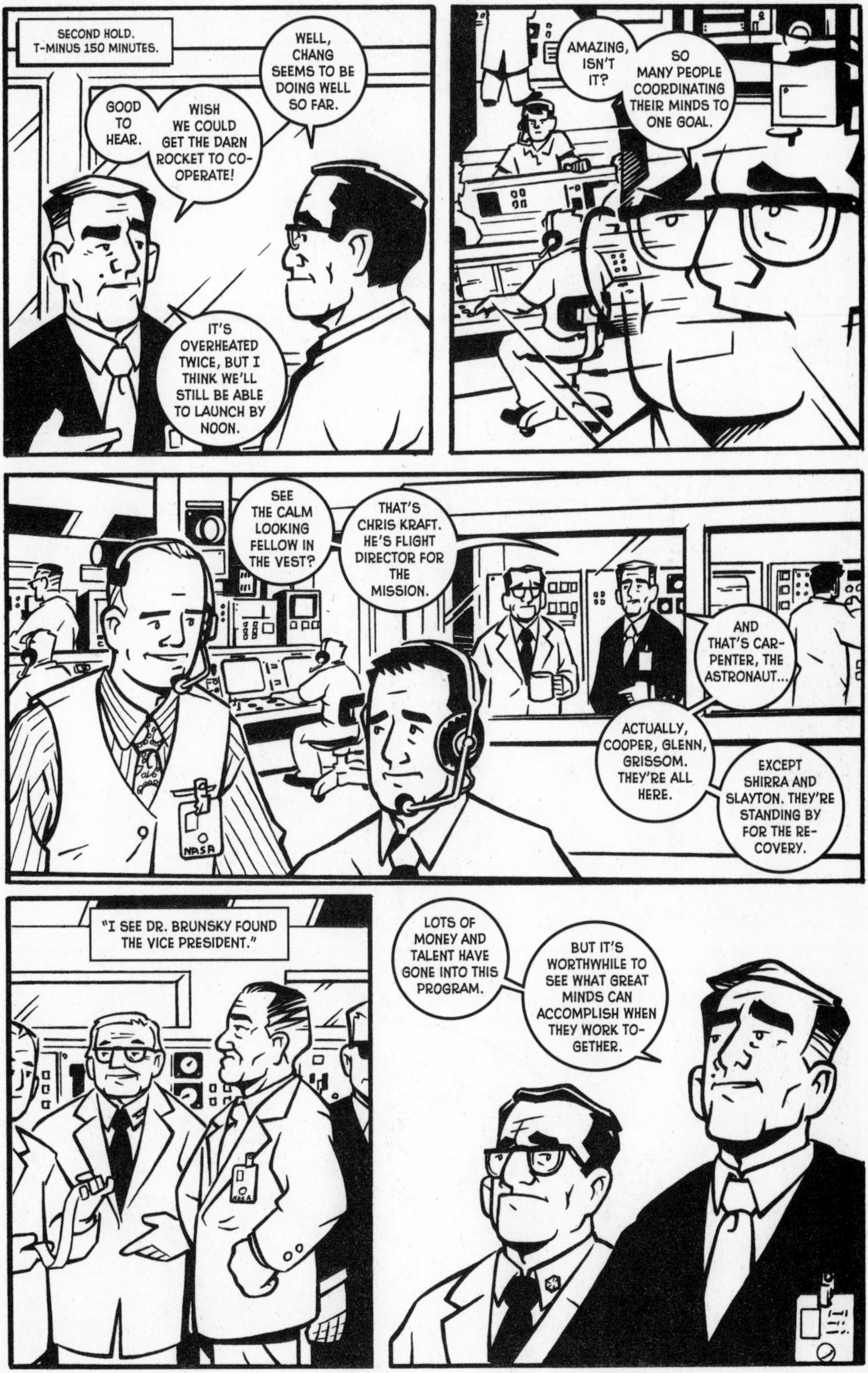
SECOND HOLD. T-MINUS 150 MINUTES.
WELL, CHANG SEEMS TO BE DOING WELL SO FAR.
GOOD TO HEAR.
WISH WE COULD GET THE DARN ROCKET TO CO-OPERATE!
IT'S OVERHEATED TWICE, BUT I THINK WE'LL STILL BE ABLE TO LAUNCH BY NOON.
AMAZING, ISN'T IT?
SO MANY PEOPLE COORDINATING THEIR MINDS TO ONE GOAL.
SEE THE CALM LOOKING FELLOW IN THE VEST?
THAT'S CHRIS KRAFT. HE'S FLIGHT DIRECTOR FOR THE MISSION.
AND THAT'S CAR-PENTER, THE ASTRONAUT...
ACTUALLY, COOPER, GLENN, GRISSOM. THEY'RE ALL HERE.
EXCEPT SHIRRA AND SLAYTON. THEY'RE STANDING BY FOR THE RE-COVERY.
NASA
"I SEE DR. BRUNSKY FOUND THE VICE PRESIDENT."
LOTS OF MONEY AND TALENT HAVE GONE INTO THIS PROGRAM.
BUT IT'S WORTHWHILE TO SEE WHAT GREAT MINDS CAN ACCOMPLISH WHEN THEY WORK TO-GETHER.

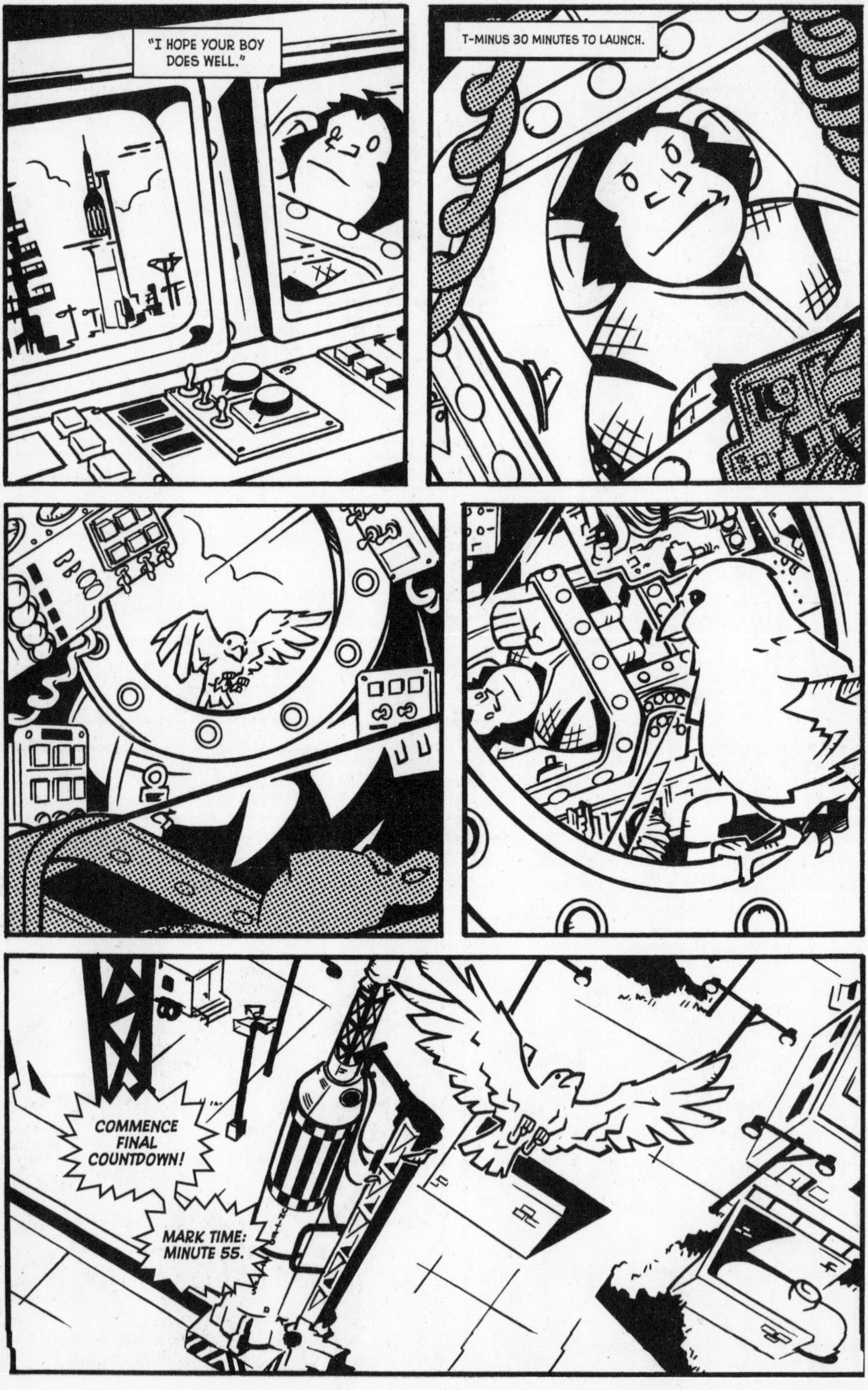
"I HOPE YOUR BOY DOES WELL."
T-MINUS 30 MINUTES TO LAUNCH.
COMMENCE FINAL COUNTDOWN!
MARK TIME: MINUTE 55.

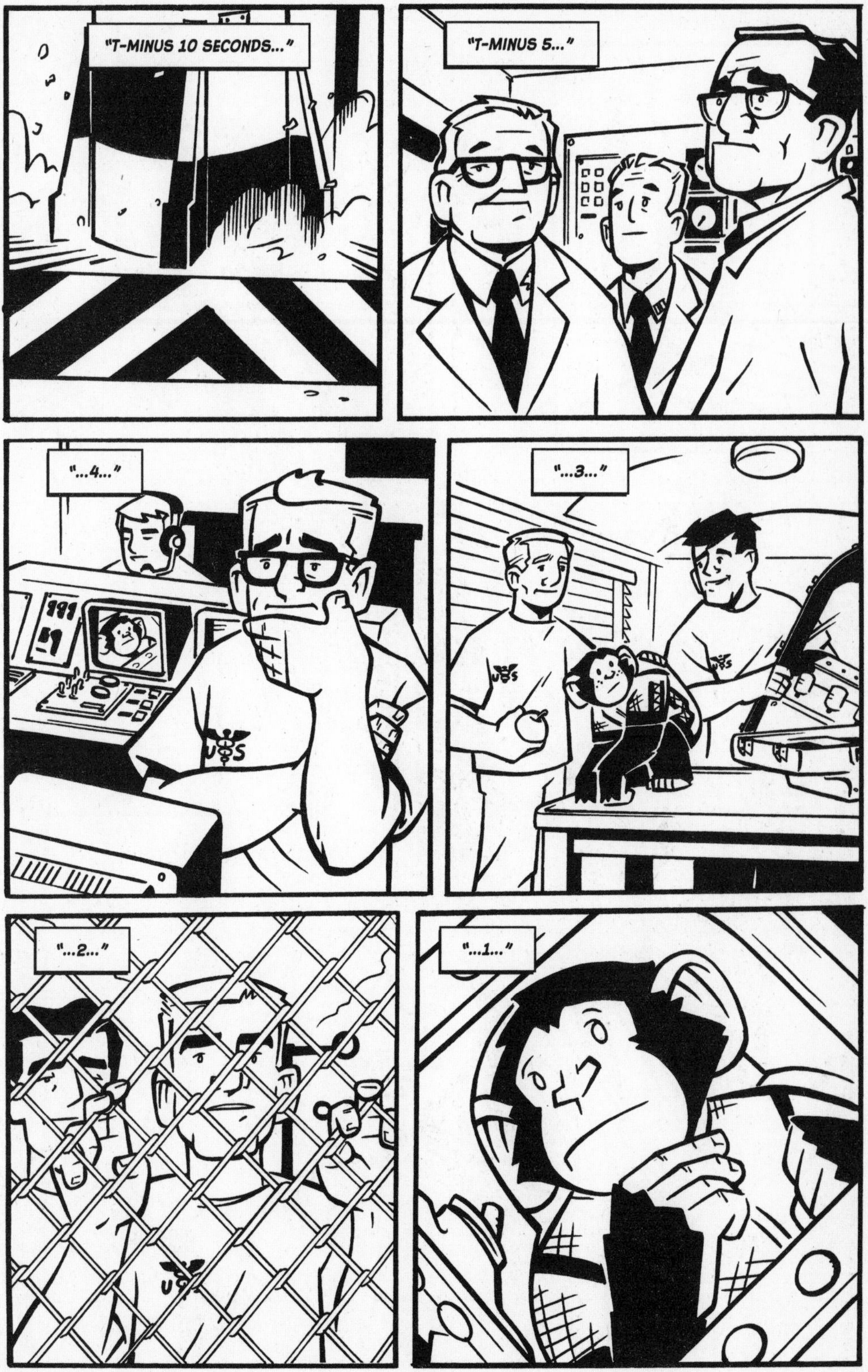
"T-MINUS 10 SECONDS..."
"T-MINUS 5..."
"...4..."
"...3..."
"...2..."
"...1..."

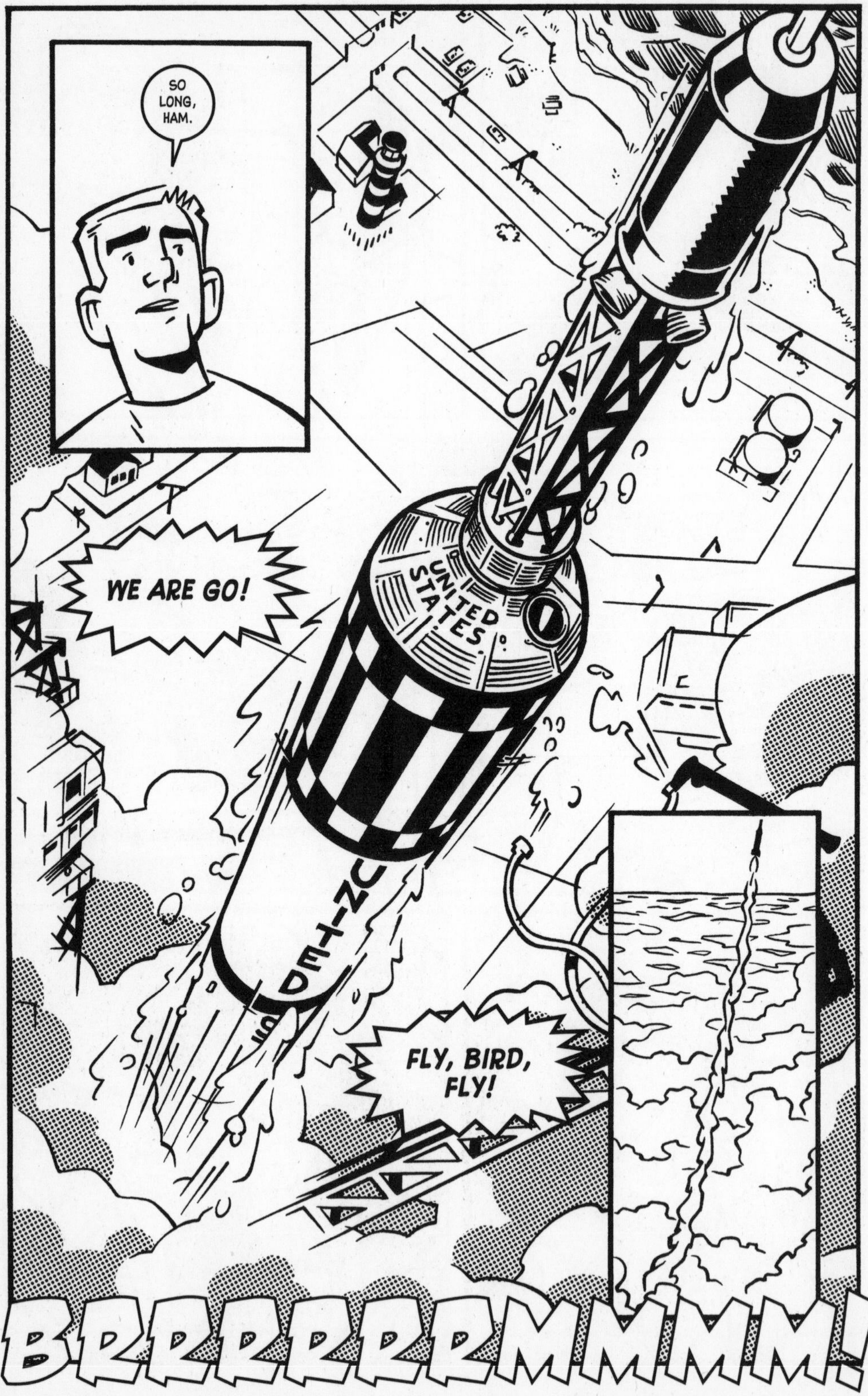
SO LONG, HAM.
WE ARE GO!
UNITED STATES
UNITED
FLY, BIRD, FLY!
BRRRRRRMMMMM!

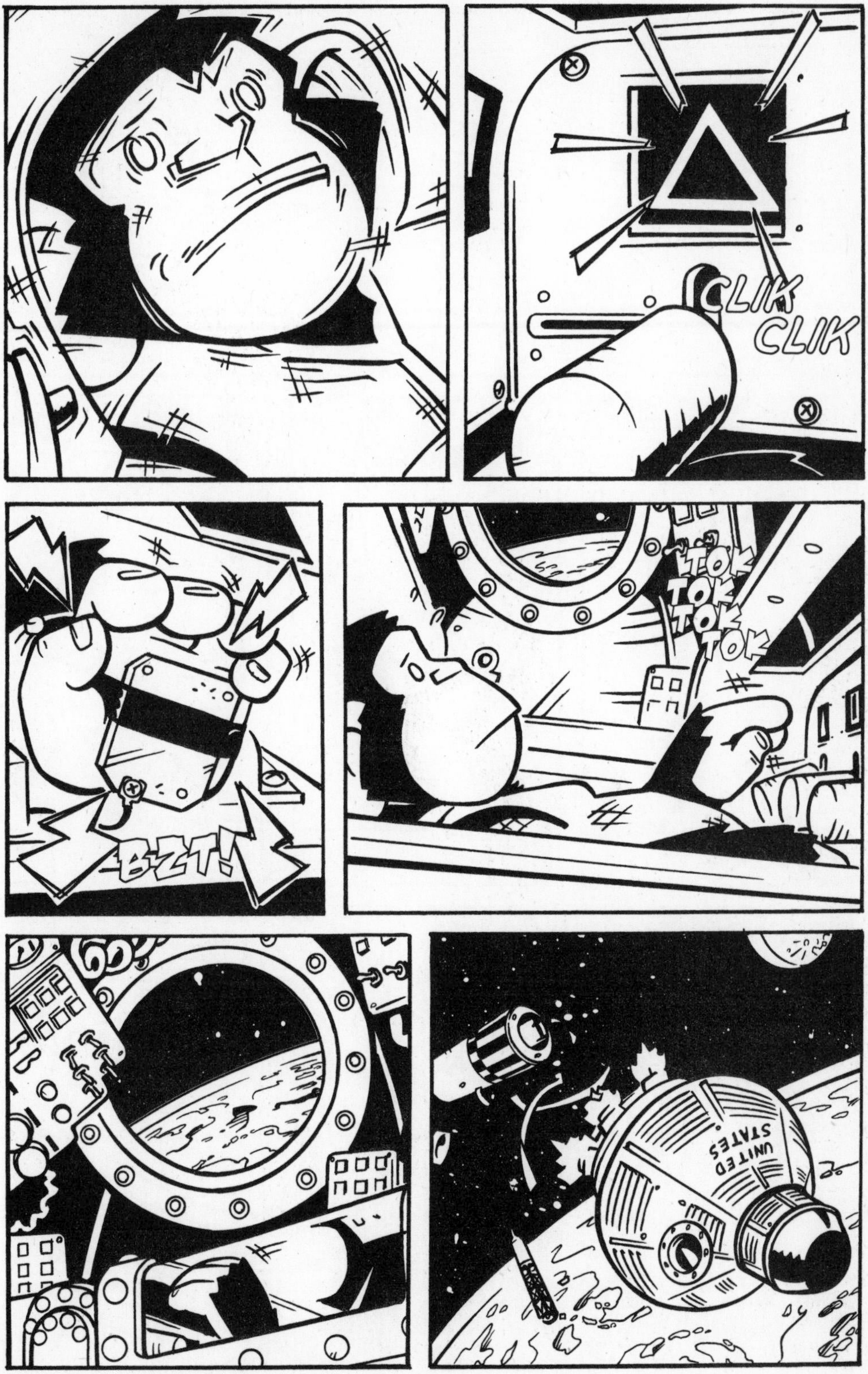
CLIK
CLIK
BZT!
TOK
TOK
TOK
TOK
UNITED
STATES

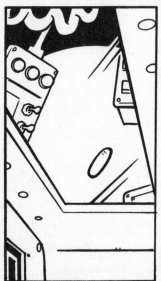

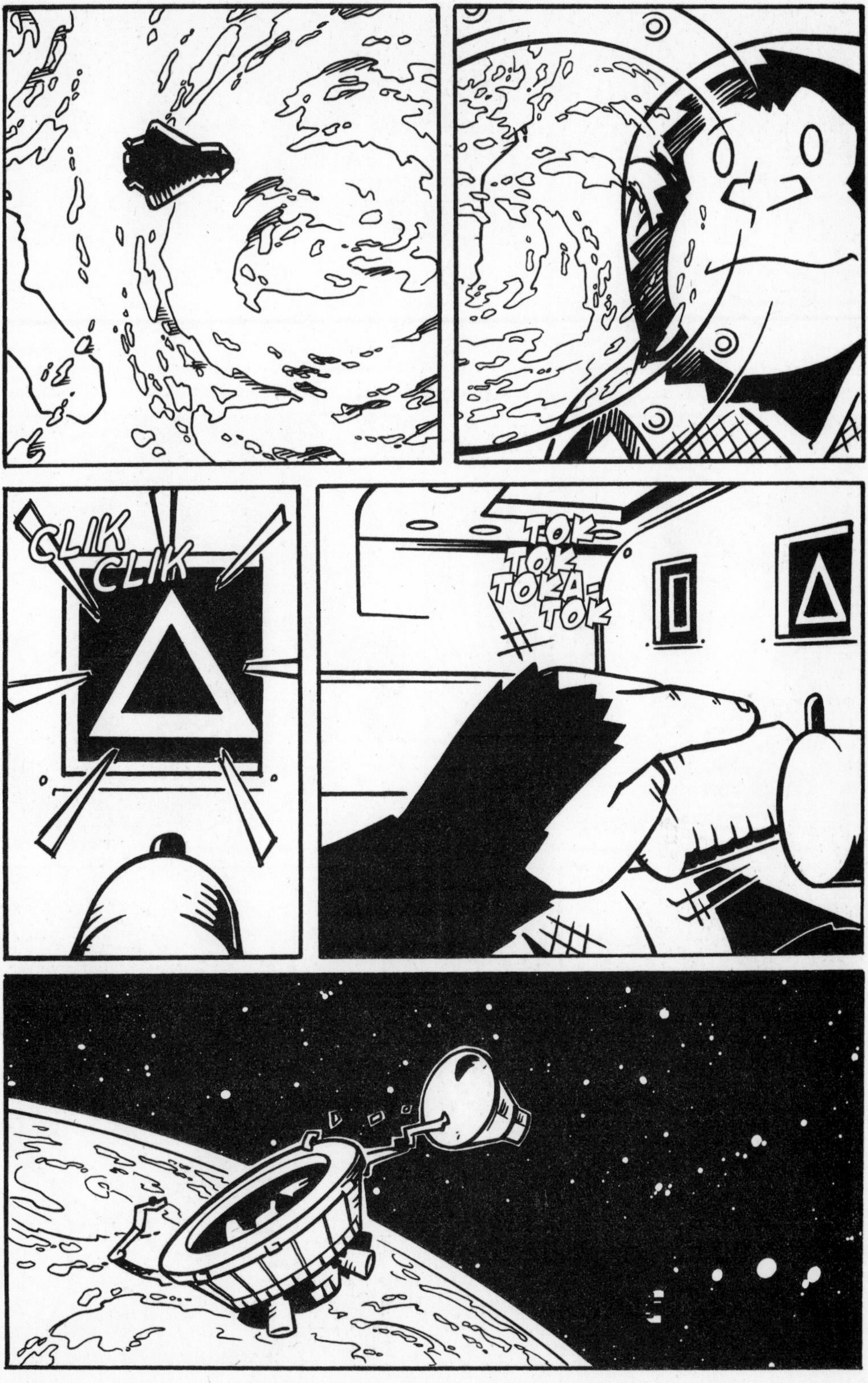
CLIK
CLIK
TOK-
TOK
TOKA-
TOK

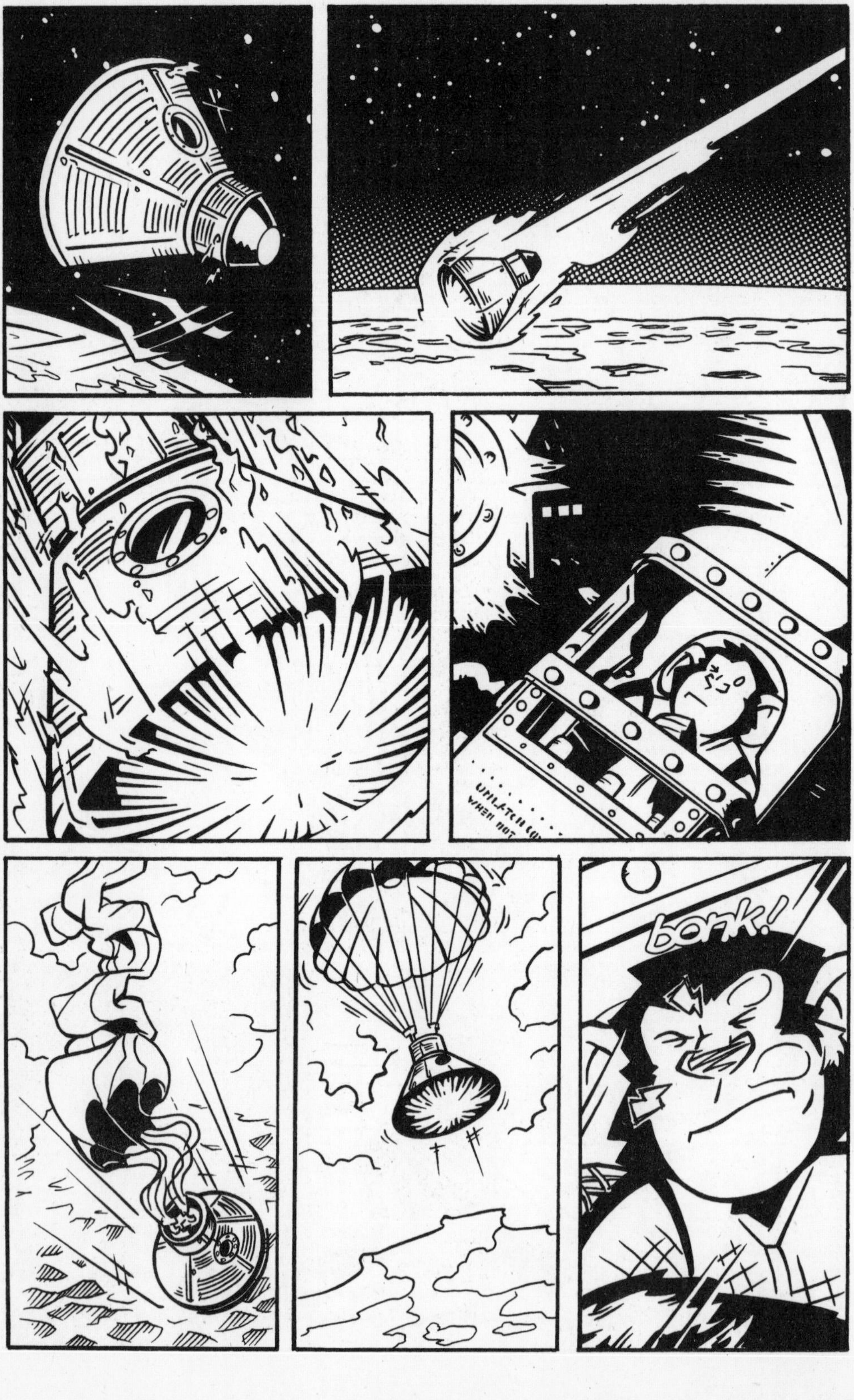
bonk!

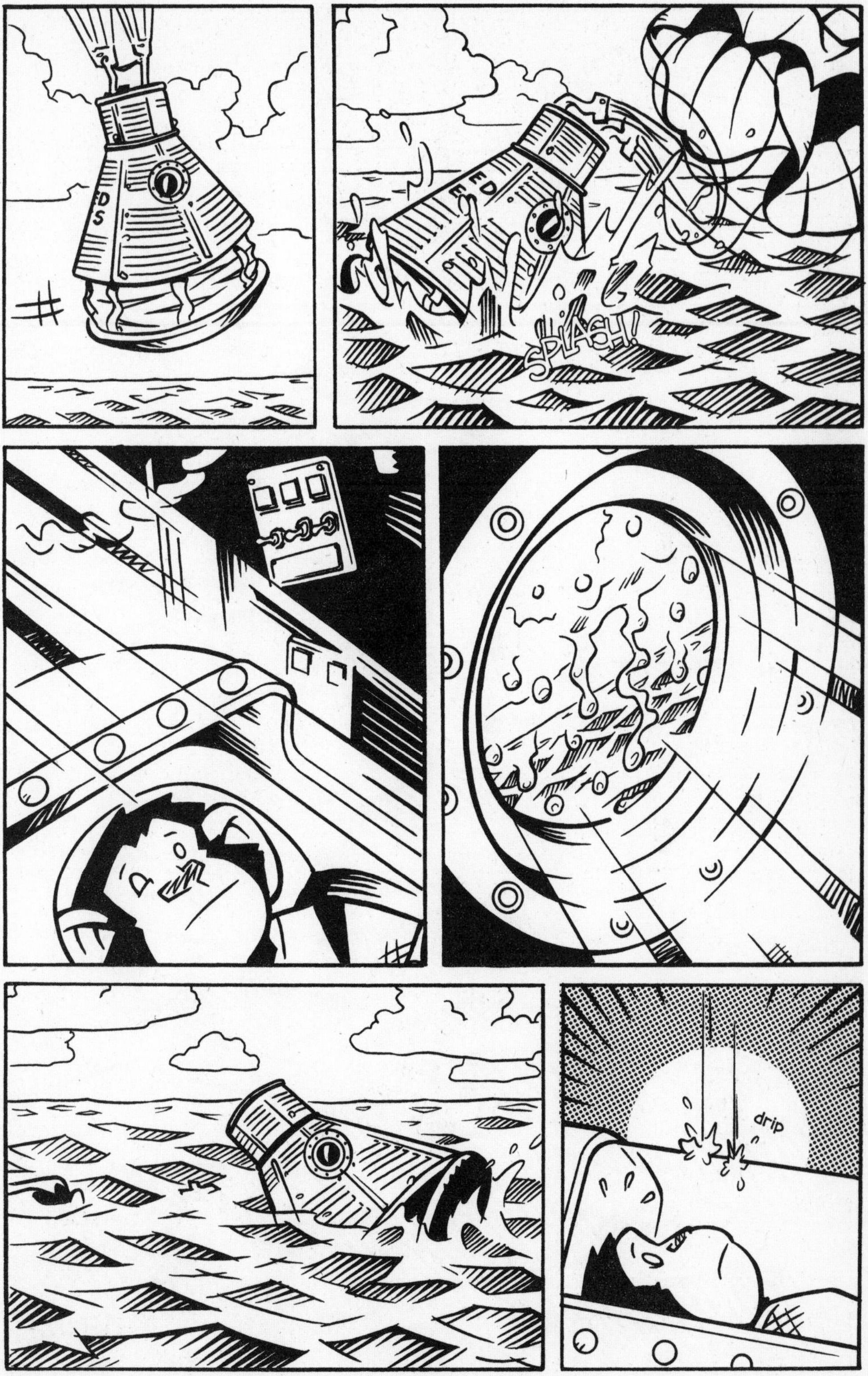
SPLASH!
drip

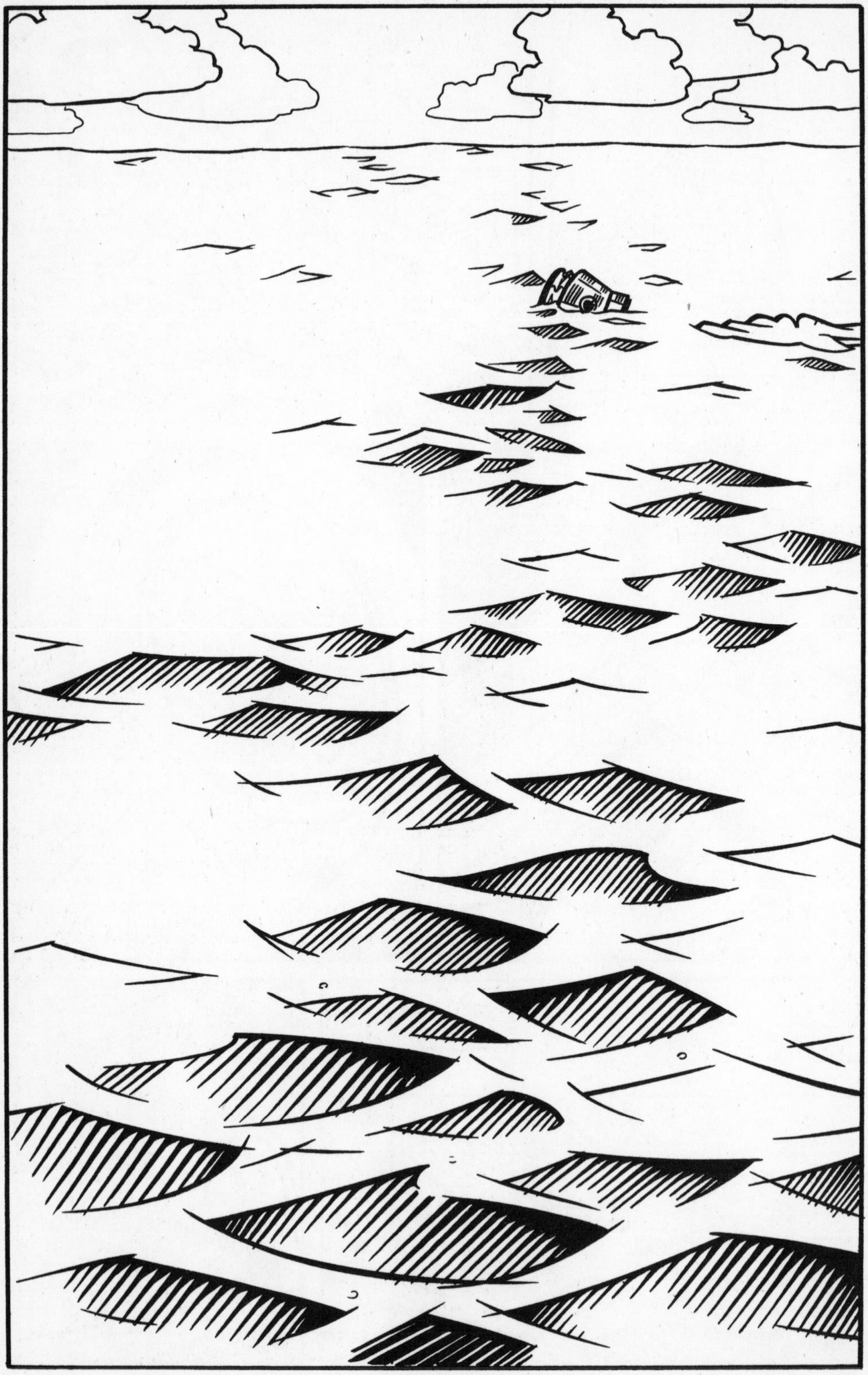

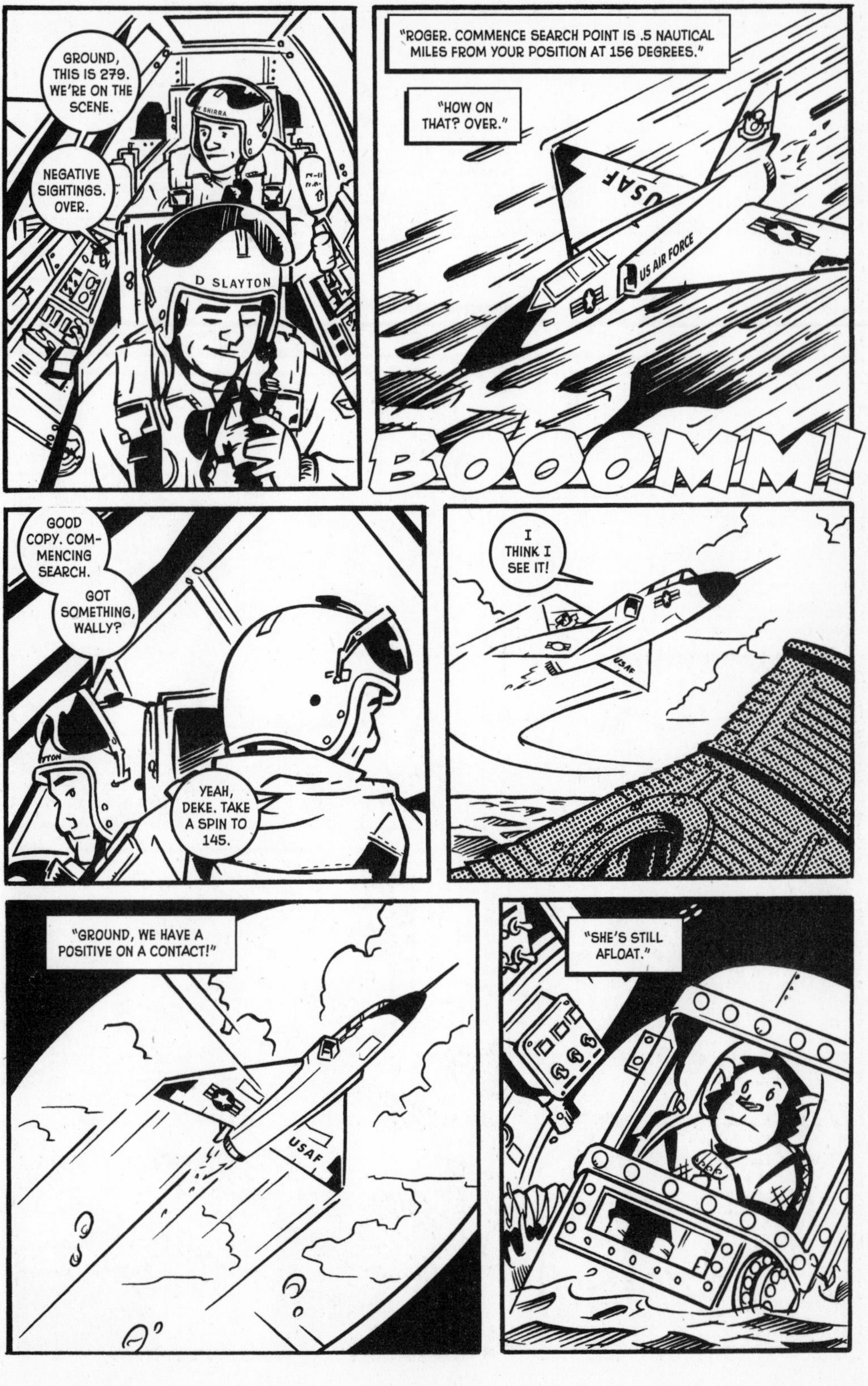
GROUND, THIS IS 279. WE'RE ON THE SCENE.
NEGATIVE SIGHTINGS. OVER.
D SLAYTON
"ROGER. COMMENCE SEARCH POINT IS .5 NAUTICAL MILES FROM YOUR POSITION AT 156 DEGREES."
"HOW ON THAT? OVER."
USAF
US AIR FORCE
BOOOMM!
GOOD COPY. COMMENCING SEARCH.
GOT SOMETHING, WALLY?
YEAH, DEKE. TAKE A SPIN TO 145.
I THINK I SEE IT!
USAF
"GROUND, WE HAVE A POSITIVE ON A CONTACT!"
USAF
"SHE'S STILL AFLOAT."

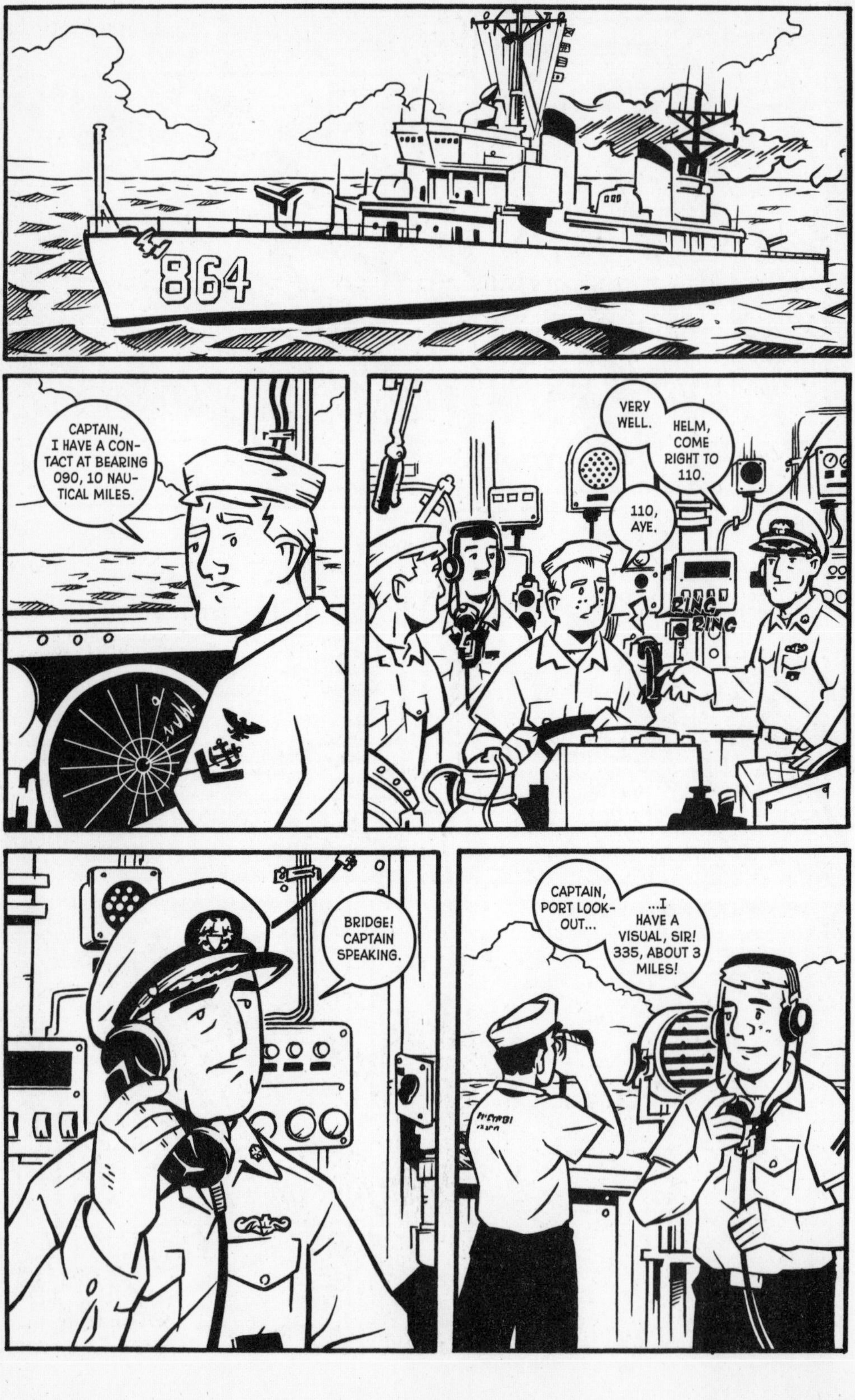
864
CAPTAIN, I HAVE A CONTACT AT BEARING 090, 10 NAUTICAL MILES.
VERY WELL.
HELM, COME RIGHT TO 110.
110, AYE.
RING RING
BRIDGE! CAPTAIN SPEAKING.
CAPTAIN, PORT LOOKOUT...
...I HAVE A VISUAL, SIR! 335, ABOUT 3 MILES!

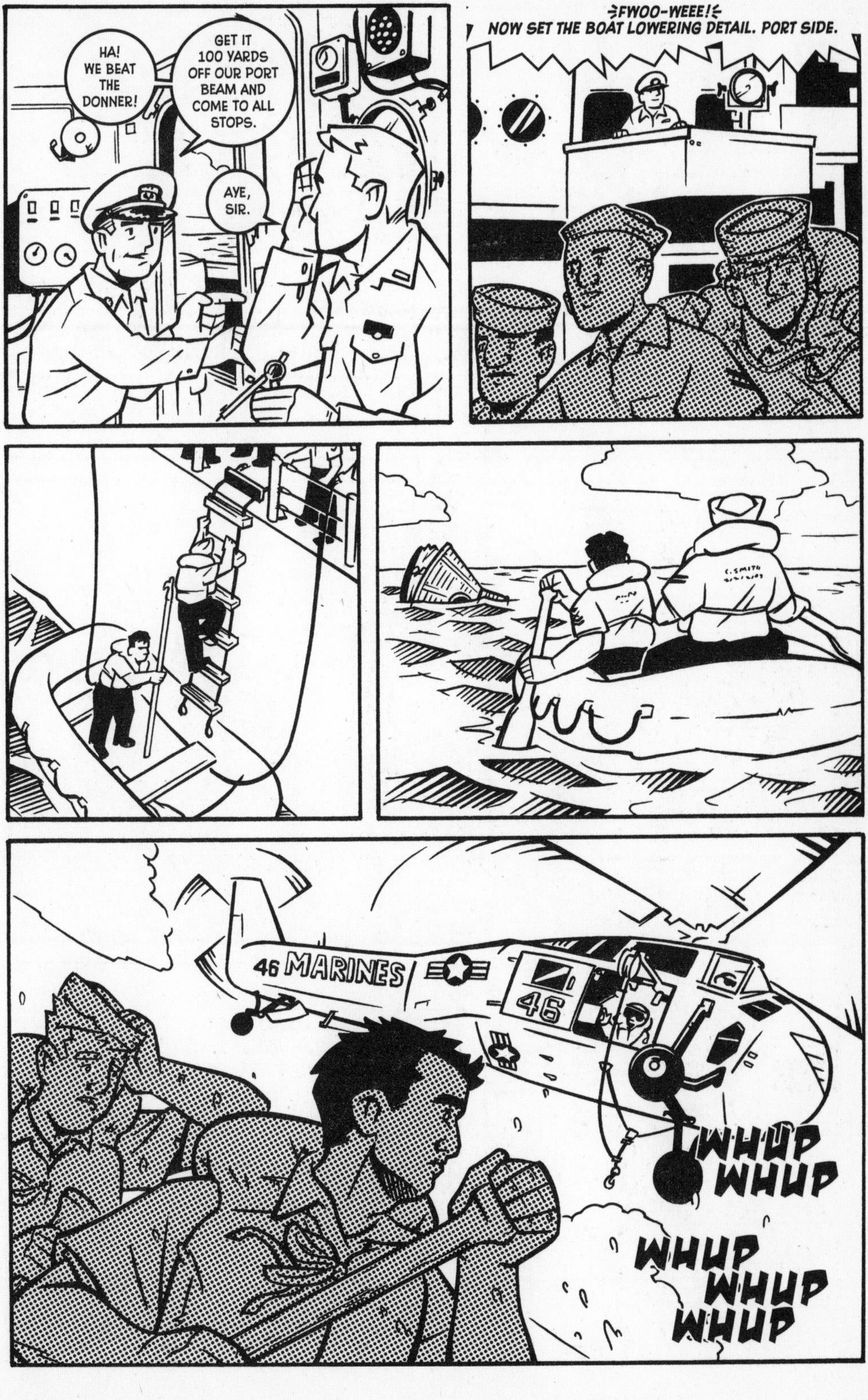
HA! WE BEAT THE DONNER!
GET IT 100 YARDS OFF OUR PORT BEAM AND COME TO ALL STOPS.
AYE, SIR.
FWOO-WEEE!
NOW SET THE BOAT LOWERING DETAIL. PORT SIDE.
46 MARINES
46
WHUP WHUP
WHUP WHUP WHUP

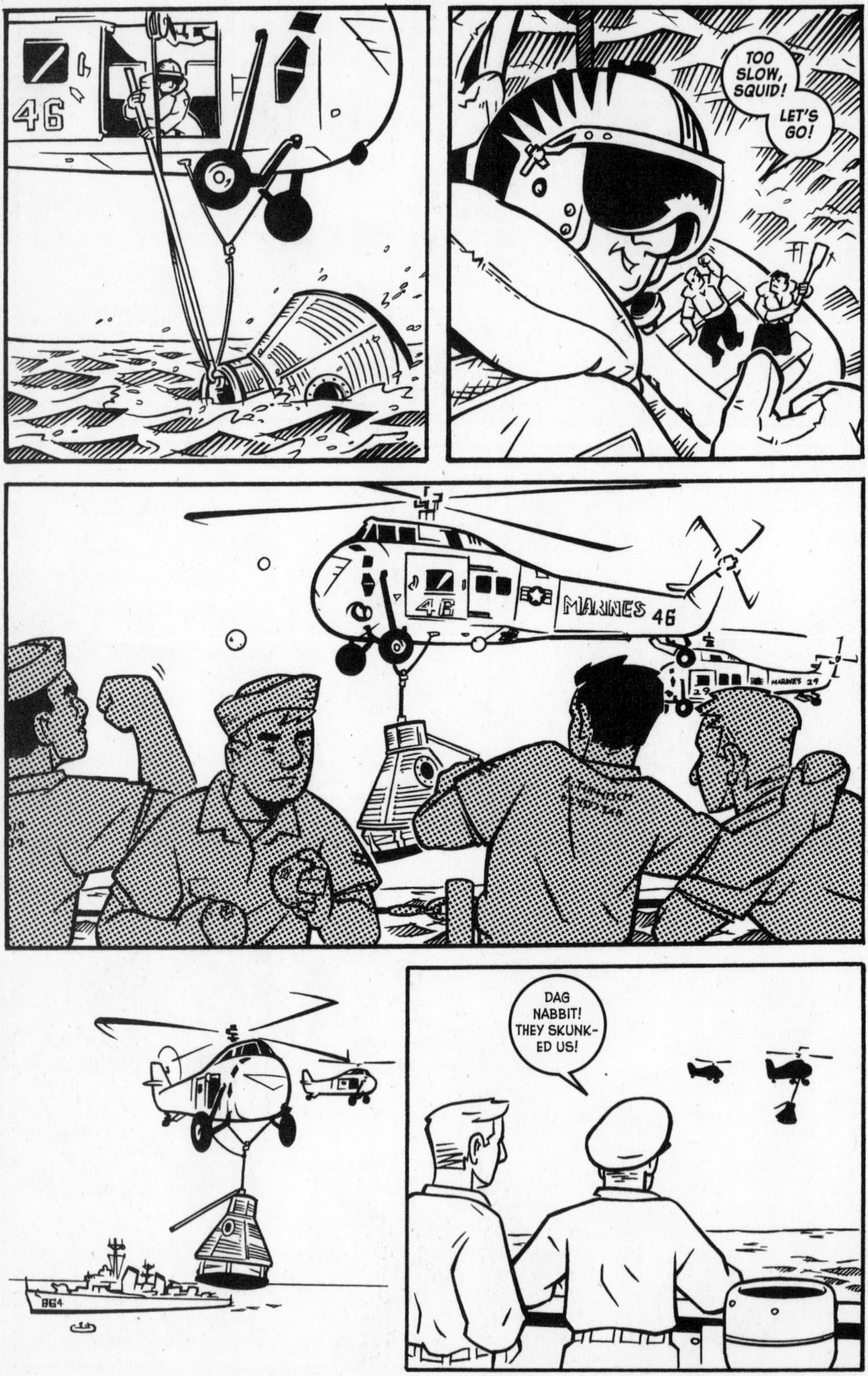
46
TOO SLOW, SQUID!
LET'S GO!
46
MARINES 46
DAG NABBIT! THEY SKUNK-ED US!
864

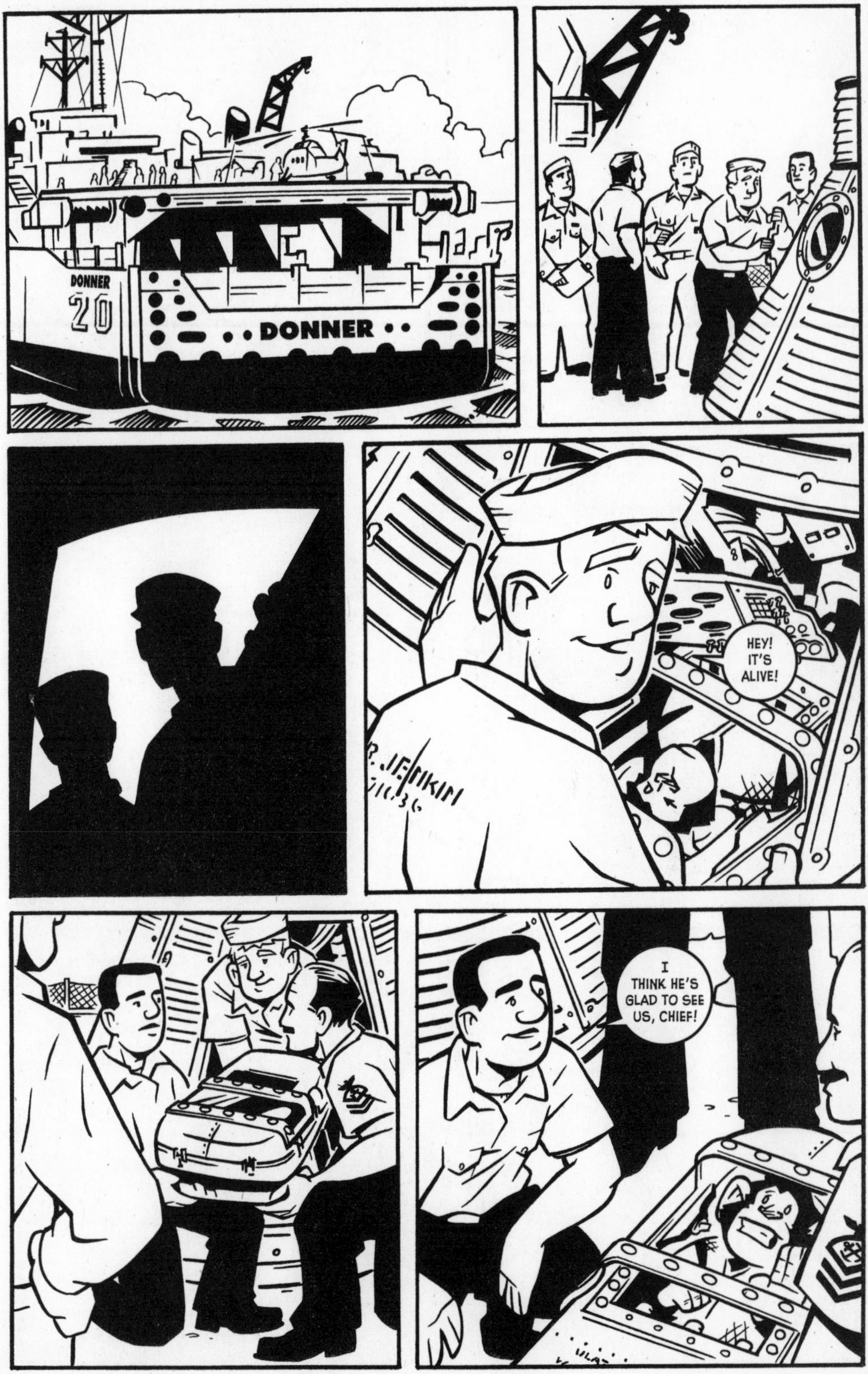
DONNER
20
DONNER
HEY! IT'S ALIVE!
I THINK HE'S GLAD TO SEE US, CHIEF!

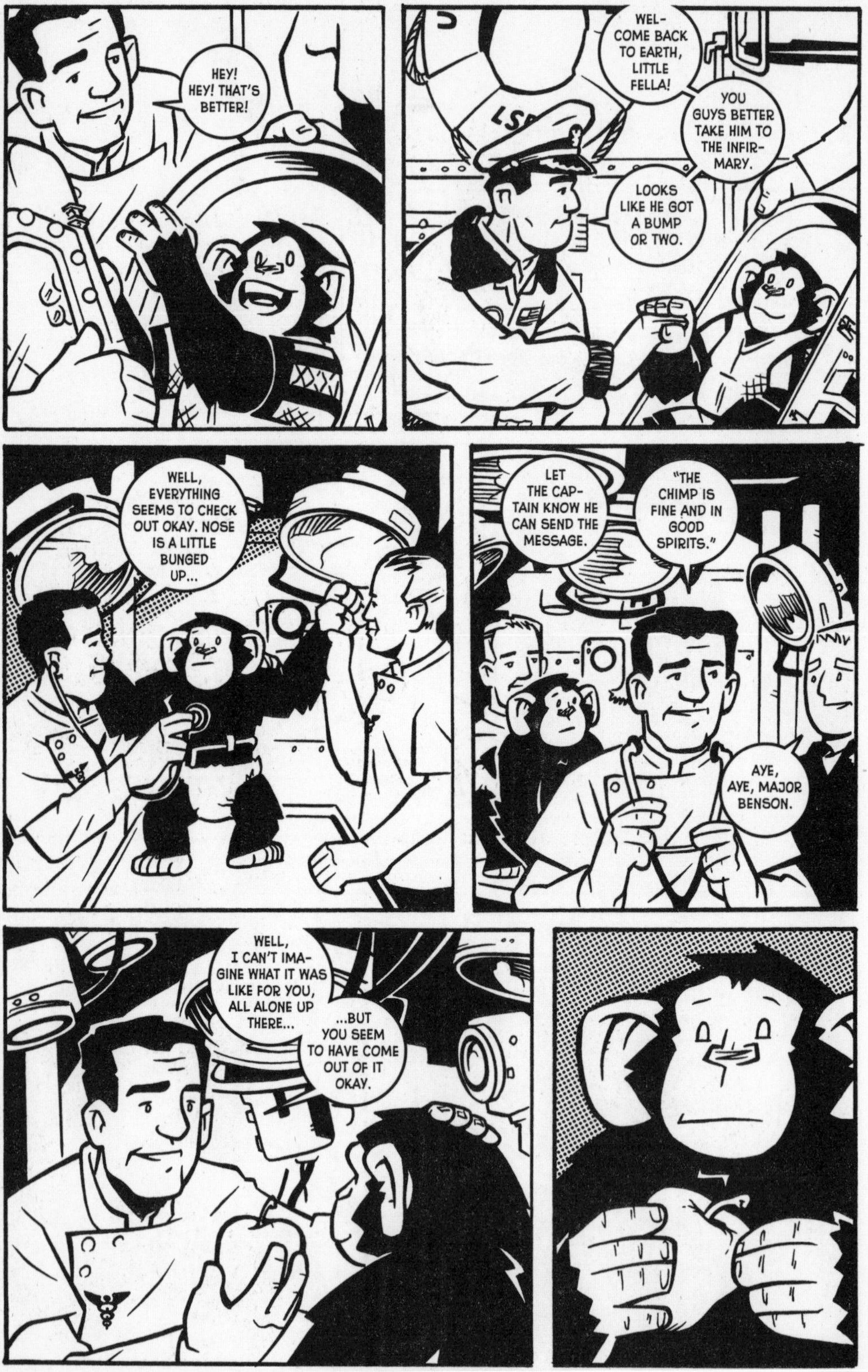
HEY! HEY! THAT'S BETTER!
WEL-COME BACK TO EARTH, LITTLE FELLA!
YOU GUYS BETTER TAKE HIM TO THE INFIR-MARY.
LOOKS LIKE HE GOT A BUMP OR TWO.
WELL, EVERYTHING SEEMS TO CHECK OUT OKAY. NOSE IS A LITTLE BUNGED UP...
LET THE CAP-TAIN KNOW HE CAN SEND THE MESSAGE.
"THE CHIMP IS FINE AND IN GOOD SPIRITS."
AYE, AYE, MAJOR BENSON.
WELL, I CAN'T IMA-GINE WHAT IT WAS LIKE FOR YOU, ALL ALONE UP THERE...
...BUT YOU SEEM TO HAVE COME OUT OF IT OKAY.

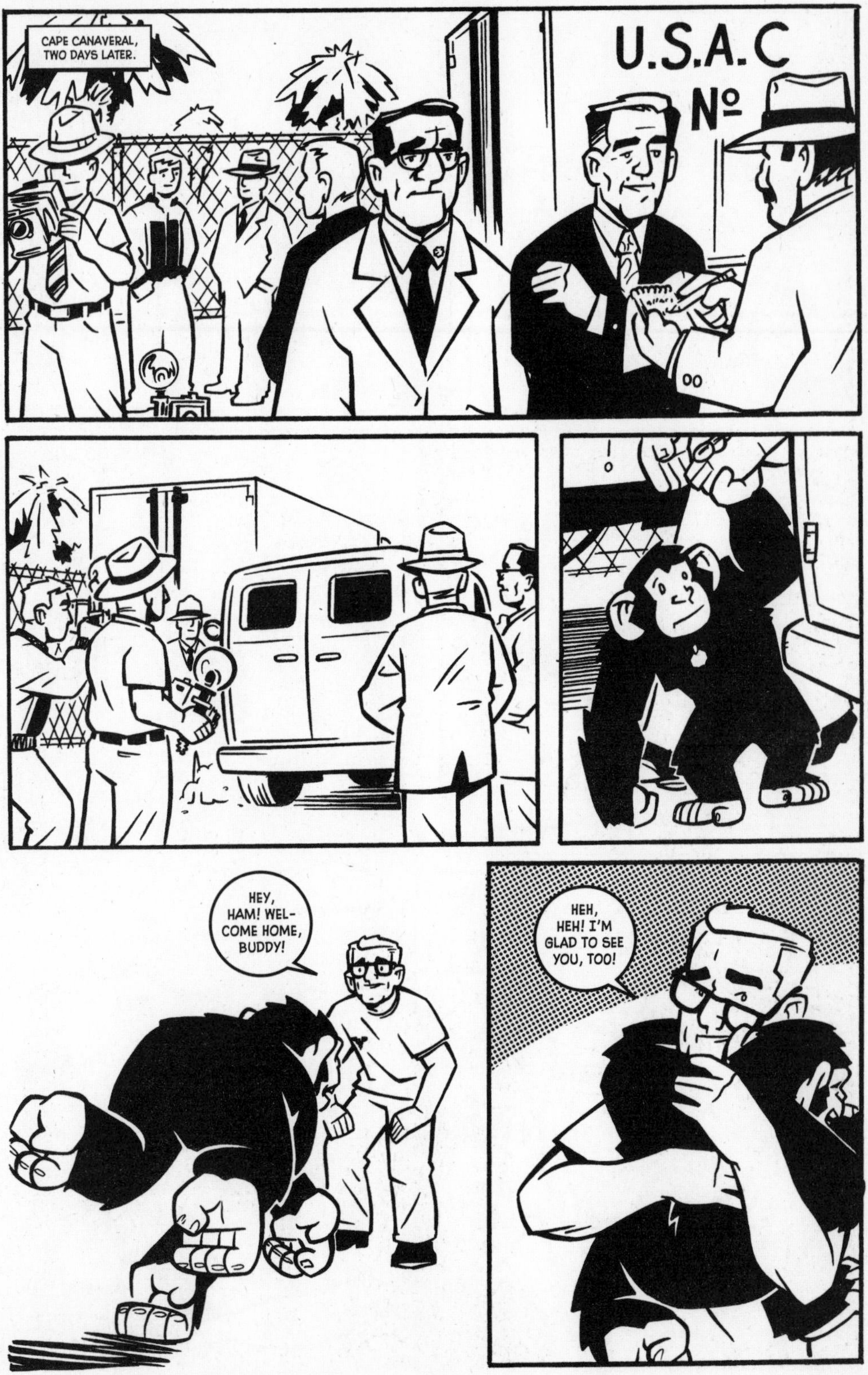
CAPE CANAVERAL, TWO DAYS LATER.
U.S.A.C
№
HEY, HAM! WELCOME HOME, BUDDY!
HEH, HEH! I'M GLAD TO SEE YOU, TOO!

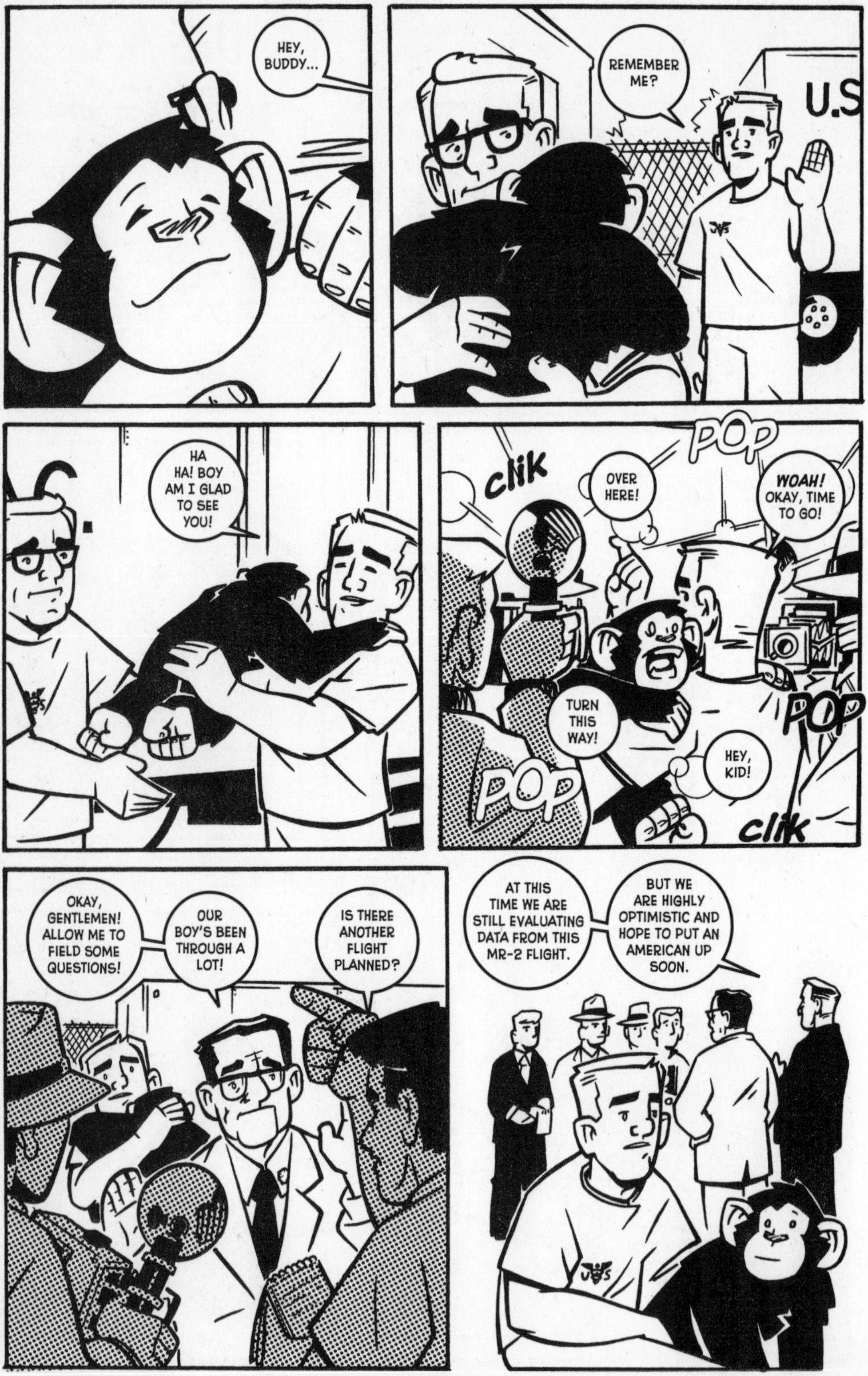
HEY, BUDDY...
REMEMBER ME?
U.S
HA HA! BOY AM I GLAD TO SEE YOU!
CLIK
POP
OVER HERE!
WOAH! OKAY, TIME TO GO!
TURN THIS WAY!
POP
HEY, KID!
POP
CLIK
OKAY, GENTLEMEN! ALLOW ME TO FIELD SOME QUESTIONS!
OUR BOY'S BEEN THROUGH A LOT!
IS THERE ANOTHER FLIGHT PLANNED?
AT THIS TIME WE ARE STILL EVALUATING DATA FROM THIS MR-2 FLIGHT.
BUT WE ARE HIGHLY OPTIMISTIC AND HOPE TO PUT AN AMERICAN UP SOON.

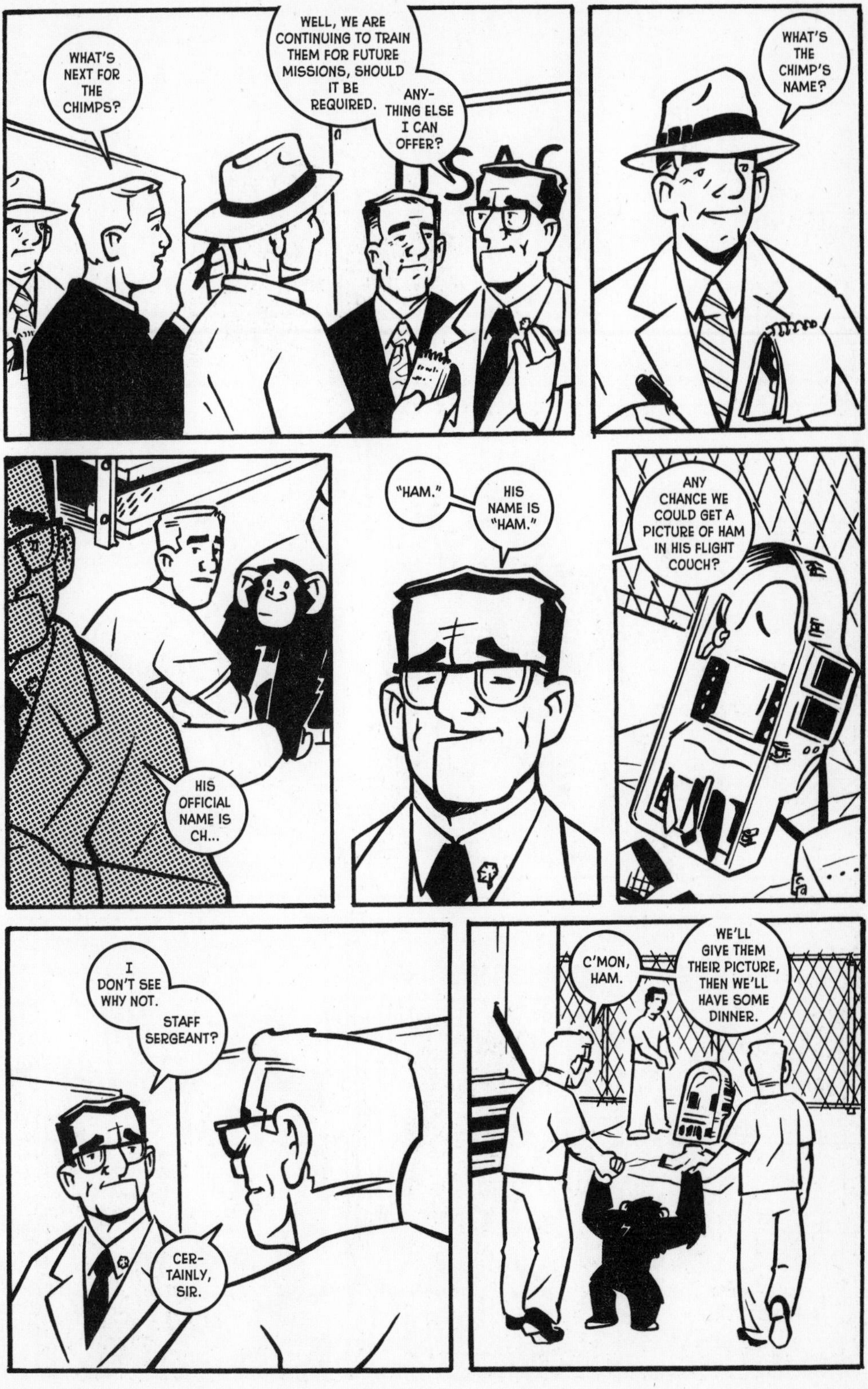
WHAT'S NEXT FOR THE CHIMPS?
WELL, WE ARE CONTINUING TO TRAIN THEM FOR FUTURE MISSIONS, SHOULD IT BE REQUIRED.
ANY-THING ELSE I CAN OFFER?
USAF
WHAT'S THE CHIMP'S NAME?
HIS OFFICIAL NAME IS CH...
"HAM."
HIS NAME IS "HAM."
ANY CHANCE WE COULD GET A PICTURE OF HAM IN HIS FLIGHT COUCH?
I DON'T SEE WHY NOT.
STAFF SERGEANT?
CER-TAINLY, SIR.
C'MON, HAM.
WE'LL GIVE THEM THEIR PICTURE, THEN WE'LL HAVE SOME DINNER.

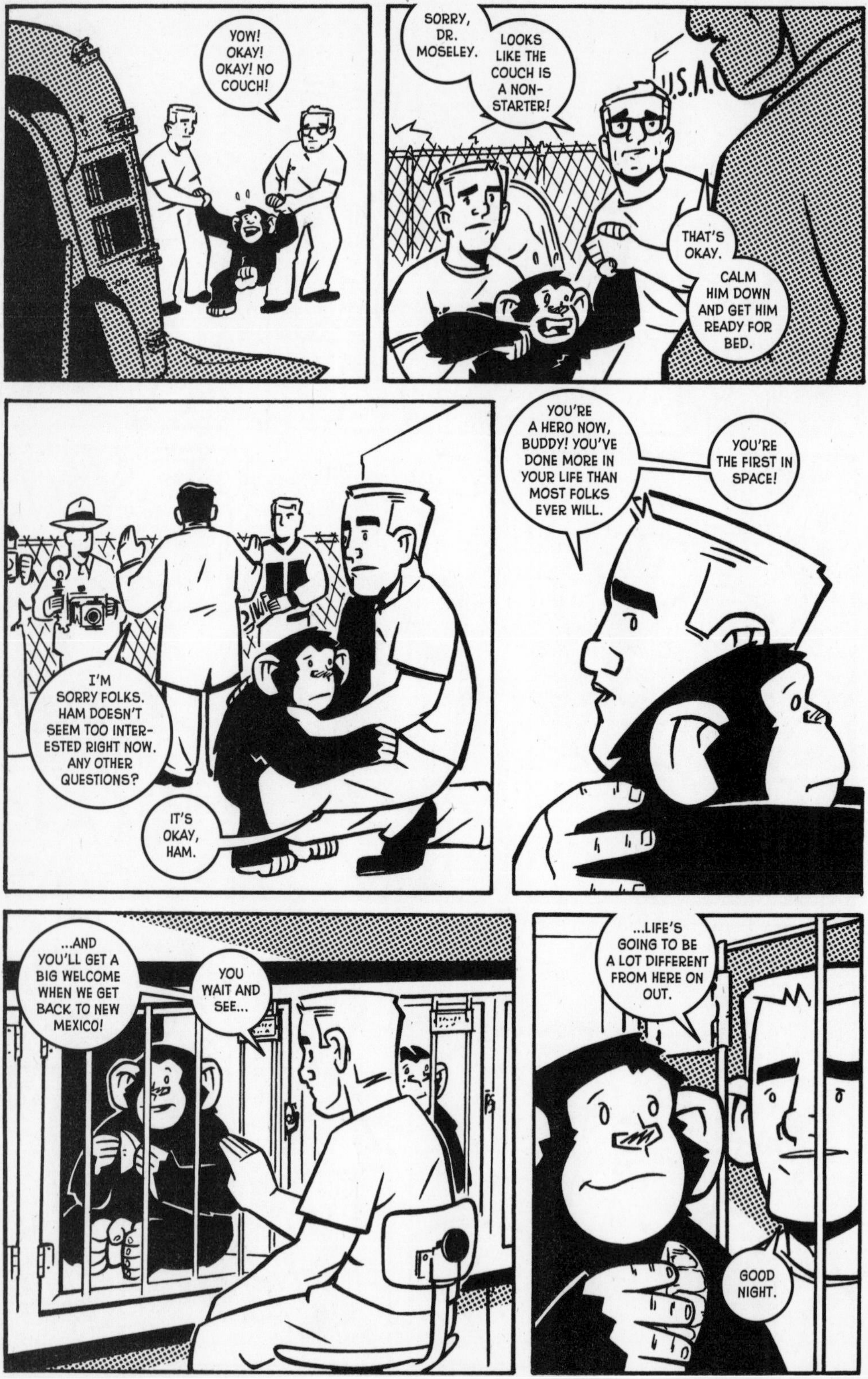
YOW! OKAY! OKAY! NO COUCH!
SORRY, DR. MOSELEY.
LOOKS LIKE THE COUCH IS A NON-STARTER!
U.S.A.
THAT'S OKAY.
CALM HIM DOWN AND GET HIM READY FOR BED.
I'M SORRY FOLKS. HAM DOESN'T SEEM TOO INTERESTED RIGHT NOW. ANY OTHER QUESTIONS?
IT'S OKAY, HAM.
YOU'RE A HERO NOW, BUDDY! YOU'VE DONE MORE IN YOUR LIFE THAN MOST FOLKS EVER WILL.
YOU'RE THE FIRST IN SPACE!
...AND YOU'LL GET A BIG WELCOME WHEN WE GET BACK TO NEW MEXICO!
YOU WAIT AND SEE...
...LIFE'S GOING TO BE A LOT DIFFERENT FROM HERE ON OUT.
GOOD NIGHT.

# EPILOGUE

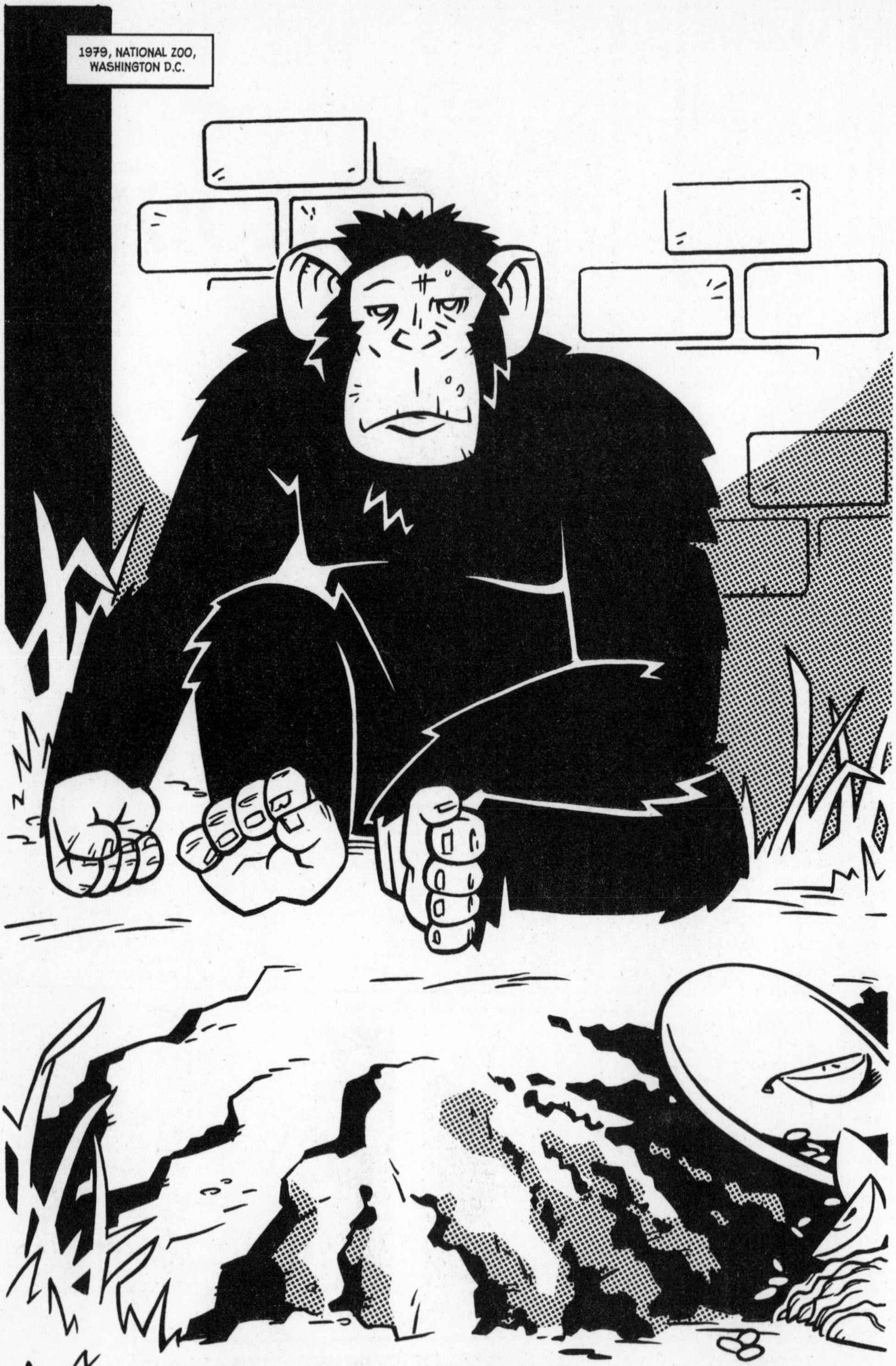
1979, NATIONAL ZOO,
WASHINGTON D.C.

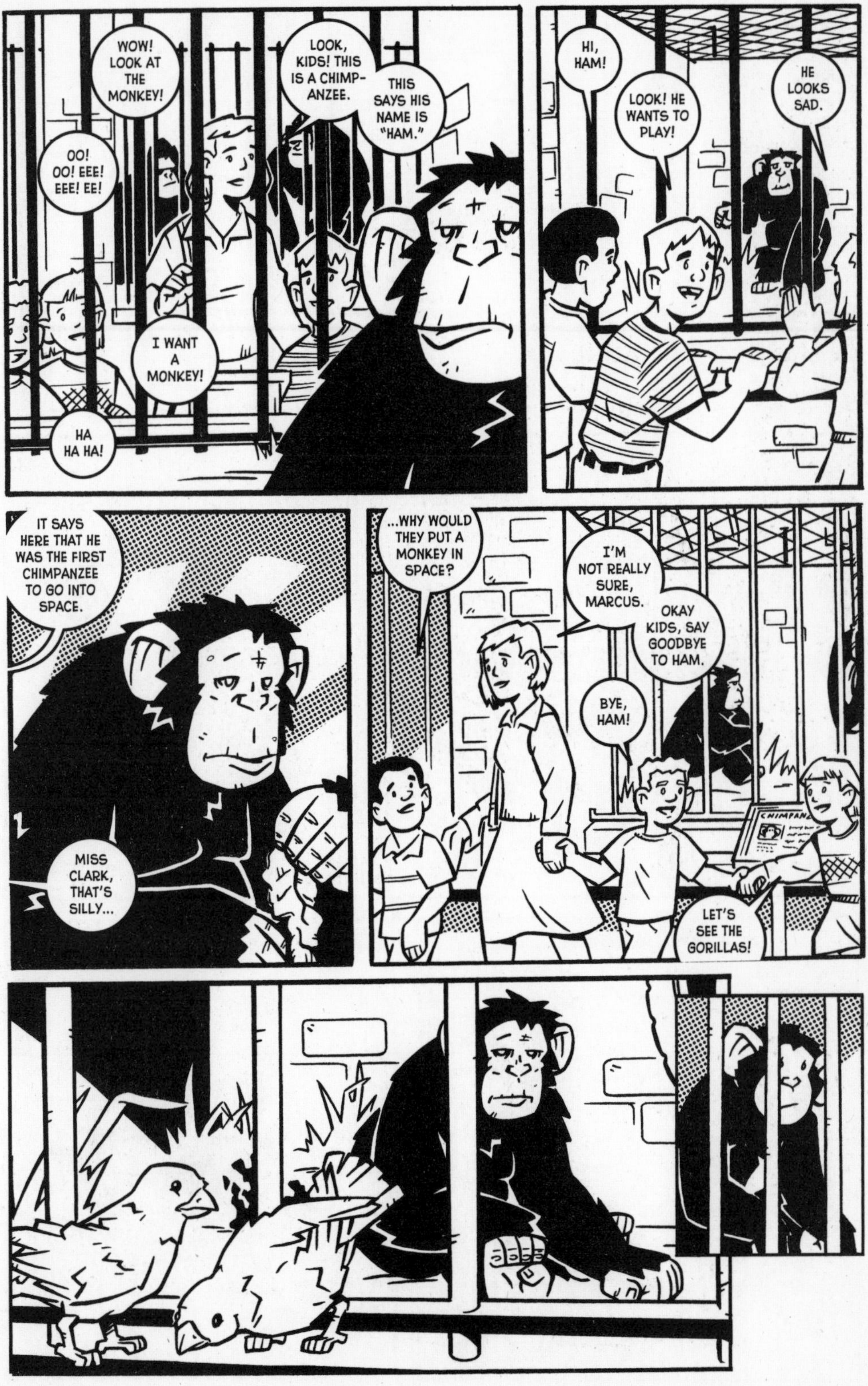
WOW! LOOK AT THE MONKEY!
OO! OO! EEE! EEE! EE!
LOOK, KIDS! THIS IS A CHIMP-ANZEE.
THIS SAYS HIS NAME IS "HAM."
I WANT A MONKEY!
HA HA HA!
HI, HAM!
LOOK! HE WANTS TO PLAY!
HE LOOKS SAD.
IT SAYS HERE THAT HE WAS THE FIRST CHIMPANZEE TO GO INTO SPACE.
MISS CLARK, THAT'S SILLY...
...WHY WOULD THEY PUT A MONKEY IN SPACE?
I'M NOT REALLY SURE, MARCUS.
OKAY KIDS, SAY GOODBYE TO HAM.
BYE, HAM!
LET'S SEE THE GORILLAS!

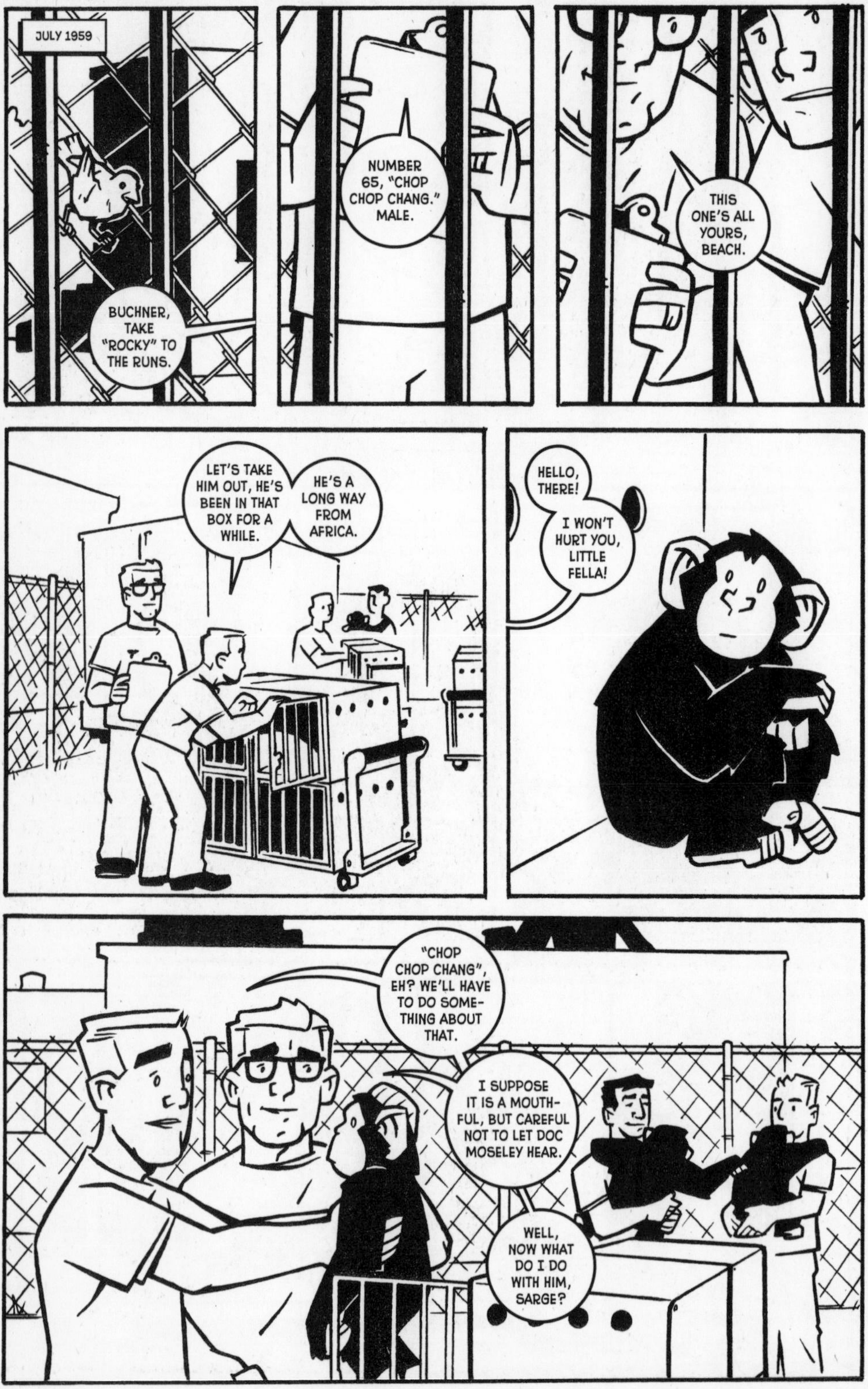
JULY 1959
BUCHNER, TAKE "ROCKY" TO THE RUNS.
NUMBER 65, "CHOP CHOP CHANG." MALE.
THIS ONE'S ALL YOURS, BEACH.
LET'S TAKE HIM OUT, HE'S BEEN IN THAT BOX FOR A WHILE.
HE'S A LONG WAY FROM AFRICA.
HELLO, THERE!
I WON'T HURT YOU, LITTLE FELLA!
"CHOP CHOP CHANG", EH? WE'LL HAVE TO DO SOME-THING ABOUT THAT.
I SUPPOSE IT IS A MOUTH-FUL, BUT CAREFUL NOT TO LET DOC MOSELEY HEAR.
WELL, NOW WHAT DO I DO WITH HIM, SARGE?

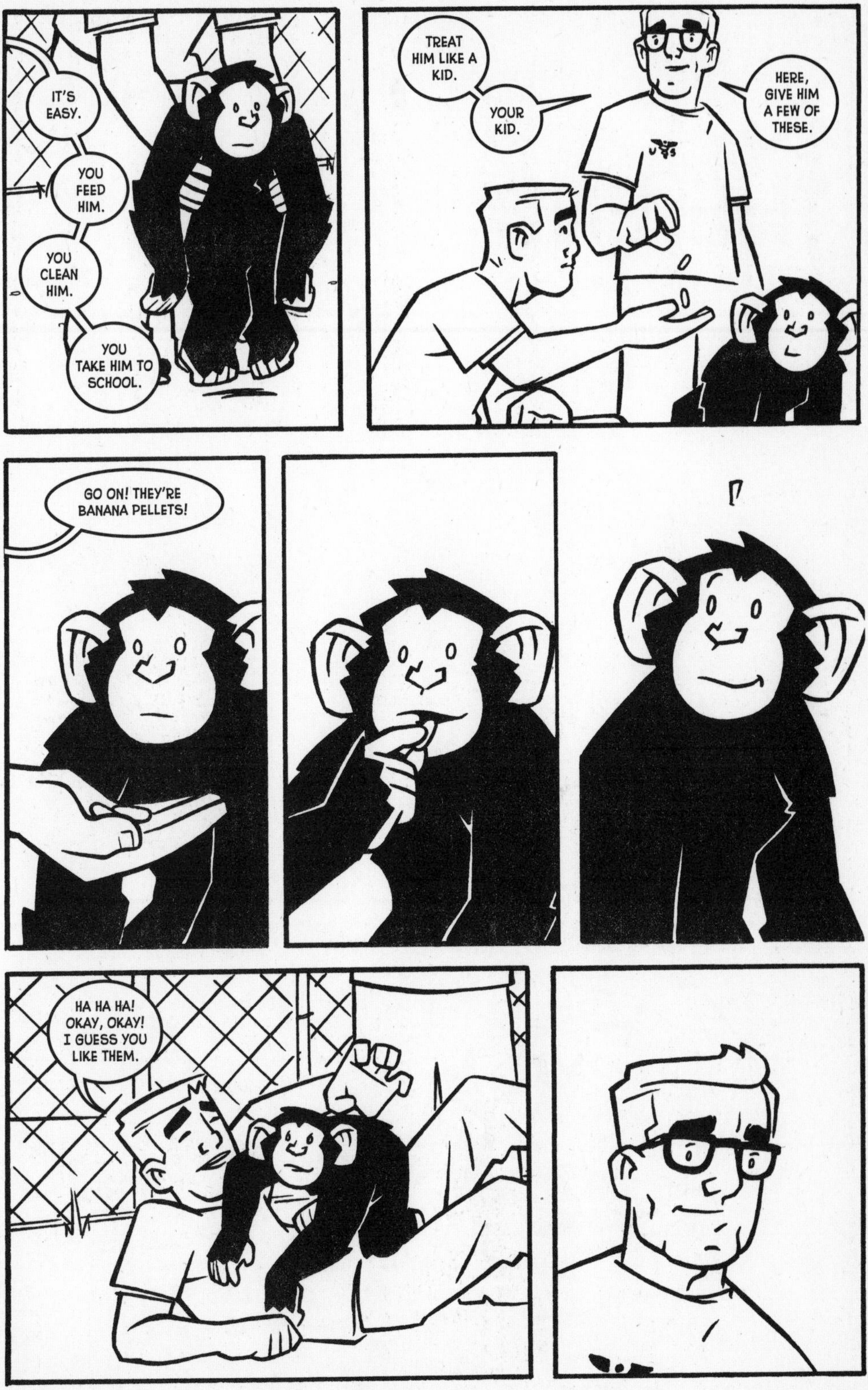
IT'S EASY.
YOU FEED HIM.
YOU CLEAN HIM.
YOU TAKE HIM TO SCHOOL.
TREAT HIM LIKE A KID.
YOUR KID.
HERE, GIVE HIM A FEW OF THESE.
GO ON! THEY'RE BANANA PELLETS!
HA HA HA! OKAY, OKAY! I GUESS YOU LIKE THEM.

# THE END

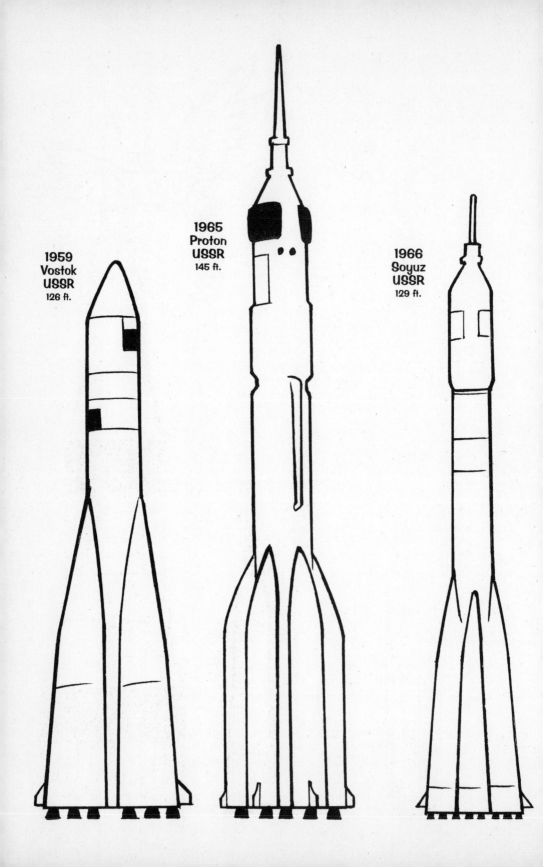

1959
Vostok
USSR
126 ft.

1965
Proton
USSR
145 ft.

1966
Soyuz
USSR
129 ft.

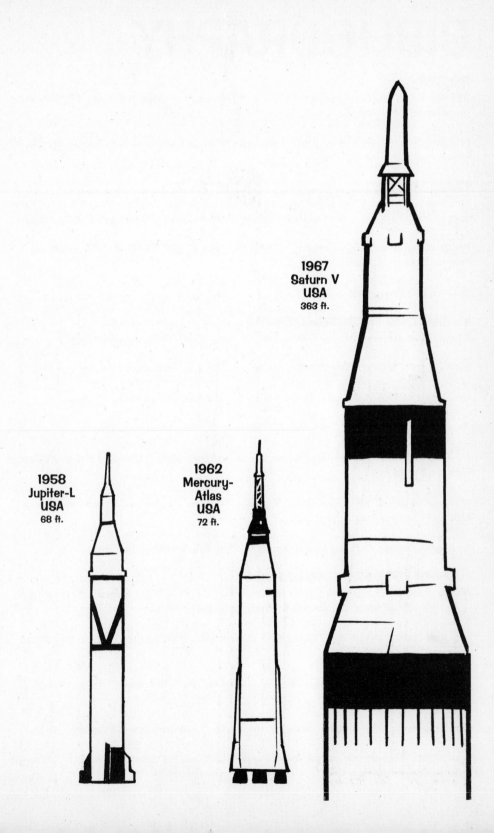

**1958**
**Jupiter-L**
**USA**
**68 ft.**

**1962**
**Mercury-**
**Atlas**
**USA**
**72 ft.**

**1967**
**Saturn V**
**USA**
**363 ft.**

# BIBLIOGRAPHY

## BOOKS

De Waal, Frans. *My Family Album: 30 Years of Primate Photography*. Berkely, CA: University of California Press, 2003.

Farbman, Melinda and Frye Gaillard. *Spacechimps: NASA's Ape in Space*. Berkely Heights, NJ: Ensow Publishers, Inc., 2000.

## FILMS/MEDIA

*One Small Step: The Story of the Space Chimps*. DVD. Directed by David Cassiday and Kristin Davy. 2003; Gainseville, FL: The Documentary Institute at the University of Florida, 2003.

*People of the Forest*. DVD. Directed by Hugo Van Lawick. 1991. Bethesda, MD: Discovery Program Enterprises, 1991.

*see also Web Resources*

## MAGAZINES (CHRONOLOGICAL)

*Time*. "Chimponauts in Training." *Time*, Vol. 73, January 20, 1961. www.time.com.

Gettings, Hal. "Manned Shot Could Come Soon." *Missiles and Rockets*, February 6, 1961.

*Life*. "From Jungles to the Lab: The Astrochimps." *Life*, Vol. 50, February 10, 1961.

*Time*. "The Nearest Thing." *Time*, Vol. 77, February 10, 1961. www.time.com.

*US News and World Report*. "Us Widens Its Lead in Space Race." *US News and World Report*, February 13, 1961.

Weaver, Kenneth F. "School for Space Monkeys." *National Geographic* Vol. 119, no. 5, May 1961. www.nationalgeographic.com.

*Newsweek*. "Where Are They Now?" *Newsweek*, Vol. 60, November 19, 1962.

## NEWSPAPERS (CHRONOLOGICAL)

Witkin, Richard. "Chimpanzee Set for Ride into Space; Rocket Flight Scheduled in Few Days -- Trip Will Last 16 Minutes." *New York Times*, January 28, 1961.

*New York Times*. "Launching of Chimp Next Week Heralds Shot by Spring." *New York Times*, January 28, 1961.

Loory, Stuart H. "Chimp Sent 155 Miles Up in Rocket." *New York Herald Tribune*, January 31, 1961.

*New York Times*. "Ship Mourns Loss of Space Trophy." *New York Times*, February 1, 1961.

Dodd, Philip. "Rocket Chimp Back Alive; Animal Blazes Trail 155 Miles High for Man." *Chicago Daily Tribune*, February 1, 1961.

*New York Times*. "Ham, the Space Chimpanzee, Bears Up Well; Flown to Canaveral to Resume Game of Lights and Levers." *New York Times*, Special to the *New York Times*, February 2, 1961.

*New York Times*. "Chimpanzee Cool to Space Harness." *New York Times*, February 3, 1961.

Hart, Sam. "Space Chimp's Future Brighter." *Newport News Daily Press*, September 1, 1979.

*New York Times*. "Ham, First Chimp in Space, Dies in Carolina Zoo at 26." *New York Times*, January 20, 1983.

Washington Post. "The Right Stuff." Washington Post, January 21, 1983.

Bell, Maya. "America's 'Space Chimps' Retired to Florida Refuge." *The Orlando Sentinel*, August 14, 2001.
http://news.nationalgeographic.com/news/2001/08/0814_wirespacechimps.html

## OTHER RESOURCES

House, George, PhD. *Interview with Edward C. Dittmer Sr*. University of New Mexico, April 29, 1987.

National Aeronautics and Space Administration. *Animal Flight Program*. Press Release no. 61-14-3, Washington DC: January 28, 1961.

## WEB RESOURCES

Knill, Mary. "History of Science Documentation in the Lyndon B. Johnson Library." *American Institute of Physics, AIP History Newsletter*, Vol. 33, Issue 1, spring 2001.
http://www.aip.org.history/newsletter/spring2001/lbj.html.

Swenson, Loyd S. Jr., James M. Grimwood, & Charles C. Alexander. *This New Ocean: A History of Project Mercury*. NASA Special Publication-4201 in the NASA History Series, 1989.
http://www.hq.nasa.gov/office/pao/History/SP-4201/toc.htm

Save the Chimps. *Saving Space Chimps*.
http://savethechimps.org/about_history.asp

Space Today Online. Monkeys and Other Animals in Space.
http://www.spacetoday.org/Astronauts/Animals/Dogs.html

Creative Commons Video.
http://www.archive.org/details/Trailblazer1
http://www.archive.org/details/1959-06-01_Space_Monkeys
http://www.archive.org/details/1960-12-22_Space_Progress
http://www.archive.org/details/Cheerios1960
http://www.archive.org/details/1961-05-08_As_World_Watched
http://www.archive.org/details/1961-05-05_Reds_Celebrate_May_Day
http://www.archive.org/details/1961-04-19_First_Pictures
http://www.archive.org/details/1961-11-30_Chimp_into_space
http://www.archive.org/details/1957-10-07_New_Moon
http://www.archive.org/details/1958-02-03_First_US_Satellite_Launched
http://www.archive.org/details/Rockets
http://creativecommons.org/licenses/publicdomain/

For more information about this book, the early Space Race, and animal testing, visit www.firstinspacecomic.com

# Save the Chimps

### SPEAKING OUT FOR THEM

After the chimp programs ended, the Air Force sold many of the surviving chimps as "surplus" to biomedical firms. Save the Chimps rescues these animals and their decendants and places them in a sanctuary where they can be chimps again.

If you would like to learn more about what happened after this story and make a contribution to Save the Chimps, visit www.savethechimps.org.

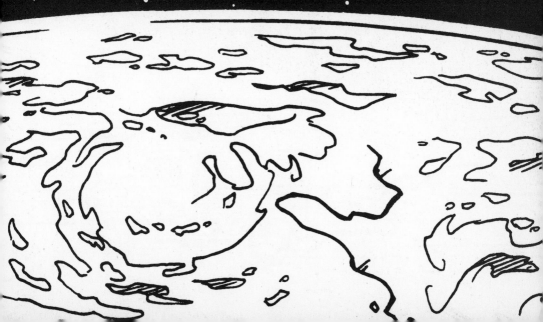

# ACKNOWLEDGEMENTS

Thanks to everyone that made this project possible.
Special thanks go to Mark Costa and Hope Davidson.

This book was written in the year after I completed
my tour of duty in the Coast Guard and would not
have been possible if not for their encouragement,
generosity, and hospitality.